LIBERATE ME, LORD

For my friend Barb. Hope you enjoy the book.

DP

Liberate Me, Lord
An Odyssey of the Mind

Book One:
The Story of the Savior, Jesus of Nazareth

David Paul

Freedom Press ॐ

WRIGHTWOOD • CALIFORNIA
2002

Copyright © 2002 David Paul

All rights reserved. Portions of this book may be quoted with proper attribution.

First Printing 2002

Front cover photo: "Bristlecone Pine" - ©1980 Gerald Allen/American West Travelogue.
Artwork: Dedication - Arthur Johnson; "The One and the Many" - Andrew Johnson

Fonts:
Titles and Headings: *Flaubert* and *Elfinstone* by Scriptorium.
Text: *Prospero,* by Tim Rolands.

Published by:

Freedom Press ॐ
PO BOX 2228
WRIGHTWOOD, CA 92397

To order this book, contact:

Bristlecone Publishing Co.
2560 Brookridge Ave
Golden Valley, Mn. 55422.
E-mail: davej@jblcompanies.com

Printed in the United States by:
Morris Publishing • 3212 East Highway 30 • Kearney, NE 68847
800 650-7888

ISBN 0-9664326-7-3

This book is dedicated to my Fishing Buddies, who are testing new waters that we might fish in the future.

The Libera Me Stanza
To Verdi's Requiem Mass

Libera me, Domine de morte aecterna in die illa tremenda, guando coeli movendi sunt et terrs, dum veneris judicare saeculeim per ignem.

Tremens facturs sum ego it times, dum discusseio venerit atque venture Ira; quando coeli movendi sunt et terra.

 Dies irae, dies illa, calamatatis et miseriaw, dies magna et amara valde, dum veneris judicare saeculum per ignem.

Requiem aeternum dona eis, Domine, it hix perfetua luceat eis.

Libera me, Domine

Giuseppi Verdi

Liberate me, O Lord, from eternal death in that awful day
When the heavens and the earth shall be shaken
When Thou shalt come to judge the world by fire.

I am seized with fear and trembling until the trial shall be at hand and the wrath to come
When the heavens and the earth shall be shaken.

That day, the day of wrath of calamity and misery, a great day and exceeding bitter
When Thou shalt come to judge the world by fire.

Eternal rest, O Lord, grant unto them, and let the light perpetual shine upon them.

Liberate me, O Lord.

Table of Contents

Part I: Introduction   1

Part II: The Dreams
    The House Dream   21
    The Jesus Dream   23
    The Mountain Dream   25
    The Oak Tree Dream   27
    Thinking About the Dreams   29

Part III: The Story of the Savior,
            Jesus of Nazareth

1. I Must Leave   35
2. Qumran   44
3. The Teacher Must Be Taught   57
4. One Year Later   82
5. Caravan Along the Silk Road   86
6. Among the Buddhists   97
7. The Lessons of the Taoists   112
8. Initiation   127
9. Return to Qumran   133
10. Rome   135
11. Bread and Circuses   144
12. Sejanus   149
13. A Healing   162

Table of Contents

14.	The Lap of Luxury	168
15.	The Lure of Money and Power	177
16.	Return to Nazareth	188
17.	The Way	192
18.	Prince of the Herods	209
19.	The Voice of the Sage	220
20.	The Powers That Be React	231
21.	The Teachings of the Way	233
22.	Out of Bondage	239

Part I

Introduction

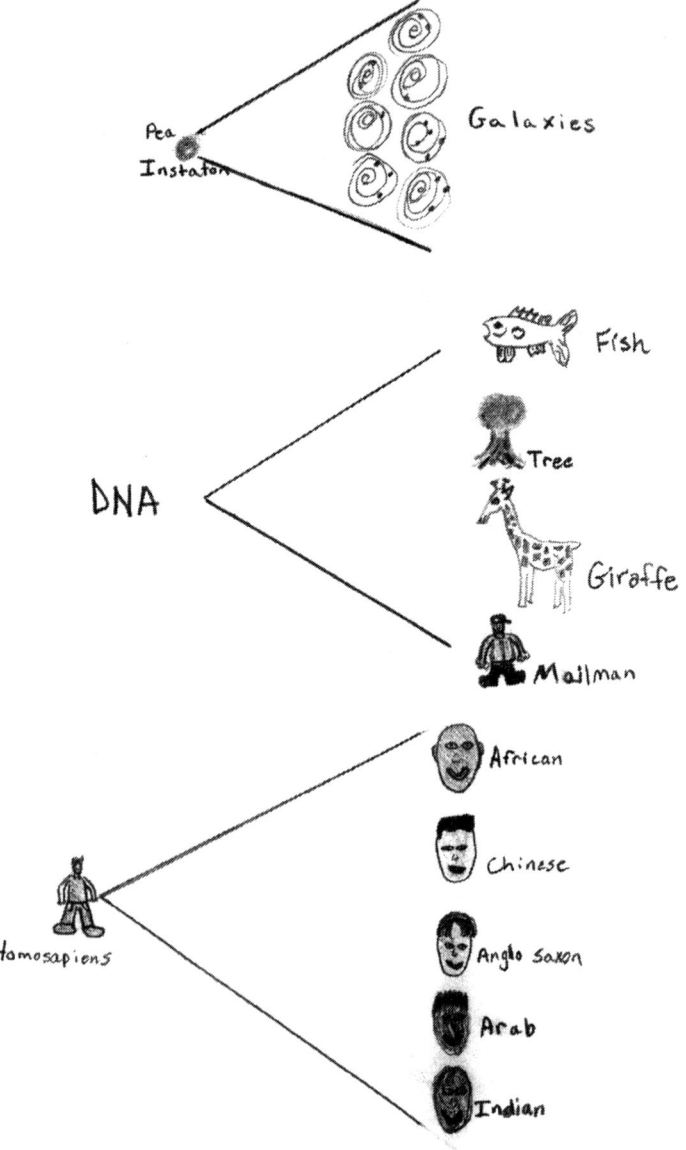

Introduction

Everything in the Universe is evolving. Everything that we know of, that is. Everything in the Universe is moving. Motion and evolution are part of time and space. If something evolves it needs time. If something moves it needs space. Are time and space causal agents? Maybe they are just along for the ride. As far as I know, nobody knows.

DNA comes to us 11.5 billion years, or so, later. This was after everything started moving and evolving. Steven Hawking's Universe started from a "Pea Instaton." Everything that there is now came from a small pea-like thing. It "banged," then inflated. Before the Pea Instaton we don't know. Physicists can only trace back in time to the microsecond before which they don't know. You could say theories of what happened before the Event are irrelevant or you could go out on a limb and theorize something that the scientific community may not accept. There are other theories of where today's Universe came from. In our world we notice things that are observable and somewhat predictable that have gone from the very small to the very large (that is by our scale of reckoning). I think that the small to large explanation sits well with people even if they don't know much about physics. "She was just a country girl but she strapped her guitar over her shoulder, headed for Nashville and look at her now. Ten gold records, movies, her own jet and handsome men all around her." The Universe could be thought of as an "enabling system."

In nearly every one of the cells in a human's body there is a nucleus. The nucleus contains strands of DNA coiled as a double helix. The segments laying along the strand are called genes. The nucleus of most cells has all the instructions to make the bearer of those cells. This is true even though it is only the germ-line cells that replicate to make baby humans. Why all the other cells have the map is curious and unknown. We have more questions than answers. There must be millions of answers to questions that we do not know how to ask. Many, including me, think that the Universe is young. It is just now becoming aware of itself through part of itself, species Homo sapiens.

When you look at the phenomena of life from the perspective of the individuated human being it seems as if one "pops" into and then "pops" out of existence. There are parallels in physics where it is noted that certain elementary particles do the same thing. Many years ago I attended a lecture by Dr. Harlow Shapely from Harvard. He was a professor of astronomy. During the lecture he suggested that one atom of hydrogen evolves into being every 10,000 or 50,000 years. From nothing to something. It is very hard to grasp for some people.

How about the Human Psyche? Why were you born into the family that you were? Why do some humans live for only 2 weeks and some live for 110 years? Why are some born into poverty and others born into wealth, the heir to the fortune? Some are born with immense talent and others are born crippled. What were you before you were born? Where will you go after you die? Huge conundrums. The fact that we ask questions and then search for answers distinguishes us from the other living organisms on Planet Earth.

People are "information processing machines." A mid 20th Century human thinker by the name of G. I. Gurdjieff said that the human machine has no one in charge. Gurdjieff left the mundane life and went on an extended "journey of discovery." Without getting too deep into Gurdjieff's philosophy we might well say that this is natural selection's human, a machine like thing. A dumbed down critter is the human machine. Homo sapiens has been speciated by biologists who notice demarcation points in evolution's wake. Giraffes are one species and Homo sapiens are another. Evolution tends to bracket its creations. There may well be "species selection" occurring contem-

Introduction

poraneously with the selection of its parts and parts of parts. Whatever is left standing at a particular moment in time are that moment's "fittest" members. It is a constantly moving front. Today's winners may well be next week's losers. The organism and the environment are in a dance. The music changes and then so do those who make the music. It certainly is different than conditions within the Pea Instaton where everything seems to be the same and not doing much of anything.

How long the Pea Instaton existed is subject to speculation. From what I know, it was a place I'd rather not be. Something caused it to explode and then expand. This was the initial creation event. At least of the incarnation that we find ourselves in now. Creation continues 15 billion years later. The Universe is young.

Dr. Richard Feynman was a Nobel Prize winning physicist. He was also one of the best teachers of physics in the 20th Century. In a series of lectures at Berkeley, California he made physics comprehendible to the layman. "Six Easy Pieces" was the title of a series intended to get the non-graduate school student up to speed. It was about "classical physics" and its offspring quantum physics. He said that all of the sciences were reducible to physics. Physics was at the base of the totem pole. Mathematics was not a science. The test of its validity was not experiment. Next in science's hierarchy came chemistry, then biology and so on up the line until we came to psychology. Psychoanalysis was perhaps more like witch doctoring. Physicists could tell you how a frog was made but they couldn't tell you why a frog jumps.

Dr. Feynman started his series off by talking about atoms. Atoms are what the Universe is made of. Atoms are what we are made of. They are constantly in motion. They can attract one another and they can repel one another.

Other physicists have theorized as to the origins of the atoms themselves. It turns out that they were made at different times and in different places. Some say the Pea contained ele-

The Story of the Savior, Jesus of Nazareth

mentary particles that eventually formed protons and neutrons as the Event cooled. Maybe 1 million years later the simple atoms known as hydrogen began forming. Giant clouds of hydrogen were coalesced by gravity. Gravity is ubiquitous. We plan things around its power. We don't, however, know what it is. Its latent power is converted by turbines at the base of dams into electrons that light our homes.

Gravity packed hydrogen atoms so tightly that part of the giant clouds became something else. Early stars were round. They still are. Gravity makes them that way. The core of these stars became thermonuclear furnaces. We live in a thermal Universe. Temperature makes a difference. A big difference. More complex atoms all the way "up" to iron are given birth in cores of stars. The foggy disks surrounding these new stars sometimes coalesce into planets. Sometimes they don't.

We "Monday Morning Quarterbacks" know that humans are eventually formed out of this soup that has been simmered just so. These humans then get smart enough to say that not all the atoms we enjoy today were made either by the prestar universe or in the cores of stars. Today's physicists note that early stars were separated while moving around, "outward", into islands called galaxies. The galaxies we see using today's most sophisticated light-collecting devices can also be described as nurseries. Humans live in a galaxy that someone named the "Milky Way." Some of the atoms that humans find on a planet known as earth revolving around a star located in the "Orion Arm" of that "Milky Way" came from incredible explosions of collapsed stars, known as Novas and Supernovas. Enough heat was generated to synthesize even more complex atoms. Complex atoms occurring on the Pale Blue Planet were not made by our local star. They were sent to us as presents by stars who died for us.

Many microbiologists refer to organic life on our planet as "carbon based." More of human poundage is carbon atoms than other atoms. Carbon manufactured in the cores of Milky

Introduction

Way stars makes up a large part of our bodies. We do have lots of hydrogen atoms in us, too, that were manufactured in the ancient Universe 14 plus billion years ago. Personally, it gives me the tingles to know what I'm made of. Physics to me is holy. My point is that we are not only creatures of our planet, but also of our galaxy and our Universe. This is true not only metaphorically but atomically. What is the Universe part of? A Multi-Verse? It could be. Cosmologists (from Cosmos) are among the most intelligent humans beings we have to learn from. Their debates with one another, on the profoundest of subjects, stimulate the neurons of just about anyone. That is if we are not too busy working to listen in. I am convinced by my life-long study of astronomy that we are more than we think we are.

Human brains are the most highly evolved things that we know of. Our perspective is from carbon-based life here on planet earth. Science has nothing to compare brains with. In fact, we are just beginning to understand brains. Do you know that there is a human being who knows 7600 books by heart? He also knows every area code, zip code and television station in the U. S. His name is Kim Peek. He was the inspiration for the character Raymond Babbitt in the movie Rain Man. The magazine Scientific American arrives in my mail once a month. I have saved all the copies dating back quite a few years. Some have been "borrowed" by friends so I can't put my fingers on every one of them. In an article about savants they mention prodigious accomplishments of others. Leslie Lemke is blind and suffers from cerebral palsy but he can play piano pieces flawlessly after hearing them once. At the age of 14 he heard Tschaikovsky's Piano Concerto No. 1 on a TV program. Several hours later he played it flawlessly. He had never had a piano lesson. Back in 1789 Benjamin Rush, "The father of American Psychiatry," wrote of Thomas Fuller whose only knowledge of mathematics was limited to counting. When asked how many seconds a man had lived by the time he was 70, Fuller took a

The Story of the Savior, Jesus of Nazareth

minute and a half to come up with the correct answer - 2,210,500,800. In addition, he had accounted for 17 leap years.

Not everything is quite so easy for savants. Their IQ's are generally between 40 and 70. They make up only a microscopic portion of the human population. They are teachers. Not only do they contribute to society with their music, art or otherwise but they teach us of the incredible capacity of our evolved brains. When challenged, the evolved brain perhaps compensates. Another part comes to the rescue. The left hemisphere of the brain is damaged. The right hemisphere acting in tandem tries to pick up the slack. The smartest of scientists and researchers studying the savant phenomena suggest "compensation" but do not know for sure. The smartest of neurosurgeons can erect a scaffolding of "consciousness" but they can't tell you what it is. Perhaps, it's because it isn't an "is" in our "classical" sense. We live and breathe in a "material" world. We tend to want to describe things as things.

Our brain is made of atoms. What vast powers lie within their quantum world? I think there are powers of the greatest magnitude. Dr. Feynman's fourth lecture in the Six Easy Pieces series was about energy. Energy is not a thing. It resides in things. He talks about the need for a "system" to replace the energy it has used to perform "work." "Work" is being used here in the physics sense. He says (paraphrasing Dr. Feynman) that the energy that can be obtained from 10 quarts of running water per second is equal to all the electrical power generated in the United States (1960ish). He went on to say that with 150 gallons of running water per minute you have enough fuel to supply all the energy consumed in the United States today. It's up to the physicists to liberate us.

Atoms contain orbiting electrons. Point particles some call them. Think of the electron as a point in space and time. They are interesting little buggers. They make choices. They can act as a particle or a wave. A wave is like a field. A particle is more like a bullet. Dr. Feynman teaches us the Quantum Me-

Introduction

chanics. Our everyday humdrum world is toppled by the mechanics of the tiniest parts of us. Experimenters shooting electrons through a tiny slit come upon the "observation" mystery. Dr. Feynman notes that when the experiment is observed by a human, the results are different from the results if the experiment were not observed. The "observer" affects the experiment. This gives rise to the realm of "possibilities." Something will in fact happen but we can only predict not be sure. The outcome is uncertain. This is a big blow to those who want to know ahead of time what will happen or to those who would like to control the outcome. There are many ways of explaining the "uncertainty principle" quantified by Werner Heisenberg. The quantum world is a world of "tendencies." The electron changes its nature as its environment changes. It is adaptable, but I wonder if it knows that it is.

Werner Heisenberg was a German physicist during Hitler's 3rd Reich. Heisenberg was a good friend of Niels Bohr. They both new that the quantum world (inside the atom) was real but it was a far different reality than the one most humans experience on Planet Earth. It became a more mystical world. This world consists of wave/particle duality. This world consists of psi fields. This world consists of nothing to something. Niels Bohr was a brilliant human being. He affected the future by helping the Americans build an atomic bomb. This bomb utilized the idea of atomic chain reactions for a destructive purpose.

Werner Heisenberg affected the future by not building an atom bomb for Adolph Hitler. Many would conclude that Adolph might have won the war of wars had he had this destructive force to control the people. Then he would create a new race of Aryans. Everybody the same. Back to the Pea Instaton. The Communist Manifesto condones despotism to get to an idealistic result. Trouble is violence begets violence. It is a chain reaction. An eye for an eye and a tooth for a tooth just plain doesn't work if you are trying to create a prosperous, happy, meaningful world of humans.

Dr. Rollo May is a student of human psychology, a teacher of human psychology and a writer of books. He probably is a lot of other things, too. He holds all kinds of credentials testifying to his grasp of the subject. He wrote a book that is of highest merit, in my opinion. I see his thoughts in the writings of Dr. Viktor Frankl, Dr. Carl Jung and Dr. William James. The book Dr. May wrote that holds our attention now is "Psychology and the Human Dilemma." Dr. May tells of his conversation with Werner Heisenberg in an automobile on their way to a conference. As far as I can tell the conversation took place in the mid to late 1950's.

Dr. May, the psychologist, asked Dr. Heisenberg, the physicist, about his "principle of indeterminacy." During the discussion, which occurs in chapter 1, Dr. Heisenberg explains that our classical, inherited view of nature, as an object "out there" is an illusion. The subject is part of the formula. The man viewing nature must be figured in. The artist figures in to the painting. The subject/object polarity is what he and Niels Bohr call the "principle of complementarity." He then paid Dr. May a compliment by saying, "of course, you psychologists in your discipline have always known this." Perhaps, the "soft sciences" do have something going for them other than witch doctoring.

Rollo May describes the Human Dilemma succinctly. The "human dilemma" is that which arises out of a man's capacity to experience himself as both subject and object at the same time. Others, according to Dr. May, have definitions. Kurt Goldstein, on the basis of his neurobiological studies, described this phenomenon as man's capacity to transcend the concrete, immediate situation of which he inescapably is a part and to think in terms of "the possible." This ability, thought Goldstein, distinguished man from the animals.

Introduction

Let's try it. "After working in the yard this afternoon, I feel clammy and look dirty," says me (the object which is sweaty and dirty). "Do you suppose that if I took a nice hot shower my spirit would improve?" says me the subject. The me subject and the me object debate whether to go back out and pull one more dandelion or take a nice hot shower. The hot shower argument wins. Competition of ideas right before our very eyes. This is not natural selection, this is called conscious selection. Envisioning the possible and choosing an alternative. We could make this little adventure more complex by adding choices. Maybe our first pick doesn't work. Then we choose another. Or we choose to forget about the whole thing. Choices that we make now can have tremendous implications months or years down the line. Then again they might prove to be of little lasting significance.

Dr. May cites philosopher, Paul Tillich, and his take on the "dilemma." He refers to the dilemma as man's "finite freedom." A succinct contradiction in terms. A paradox if you will. Reinhold Niebuhr, from a theological viewpoint, suggests that the human experience combines both "nature" and "spirit." Niebuhr's thoughts bring me to the smartest of physicists who have trouble defining "matter" and "energy." It seems to me that if it were not for energy we wouldn't be defining matter in the first place.

Dr. May now pays homage to the artist (artisan?). This one "feels" the dilemma and searches for creative ways to express it. Some 16000 to 30000 years ago in the south of France, artisan painters laid on their backs and drew glorious pictures of their cousins, the mammals. The painter's world was interwoven with that of his beasts of burden, the beasts he ate, the beasts whose milk he drank, the beasts whose skin he wore to keep him warm, and the beasts he sacrificed to God.

Eugene O'Neill the playwright describes the dilemma in tragic terms. It is the "force" of biological determinism and man's often-inept attempt to mold or govern that "force." The

The Story of the Savior, Jesus of Nazareth

Greeks, in their wonderful plays performed in the open air, elucidated theatrically the fine line between tragedy and comedy. The actors wore interchangeable masks. One mask was smiling. Just give it a 180-degree turn and the face was frowning.

To this day there are many physicists that will not accept the uncertain mechanics of quanta. The fundamentalists desire a "Clockwork Universe." This is a Universe that you can count on. Their daily planner is full for the next two years. Any deviation from the schedule affects the digestive system. You know what? On a certain "scale" we do have somewhat of a "Clockwork Universe." In our lifetimes we can count on Polaris as being the North Star. If we are ancient mariners, that knowledge is sometimes life-saving knowledge. At some time in the future, Polaris will no longer be the North Star. If we lived in a different solar system in the Milky Way, Polaris would not be the North Star. We can count on gravity, at least in my hometown. Get outside of our Galaxy and gravity might confuse you a little. Get off our Pale Blue Planet by a few miles and it will confuse you. Motion is for sure but orbits are imprecise. The orbits of the planets around the Sun are changing. At some time in the future we will start losing planets. It's like the straw that broke the camels back. By adding one little bit of complexity (the straw) the 750 pounds of straws that were there before became too much for the camel. The eccentric orbit of a planet will one day have the angular momentum necessary to overcome subtle gravity.

Physics is at the base of natures' hierarchy. Every science is reducible to physics (kind of). "Hier" doesn't necessarily mean "better," however. Why is it that the things that matter to us humans the most have nothing to do with physics? The things which matter to us the most seem to have to do with our feelings and emotions. They are not really things. The current state of our psyche seems to be the most important thing to us. That psyche interacts with the nature that it is a part of. An atomic size person sees nothing but atoms. This cluster over

Introduction

here might be a little thicker than that cluster over there. Feelings and emotions, in my view, determine which mask we wear in our real Greek comedy/tragedy. Next we ask the question: can we affect the play in which we are the actors and actresses, so that in Act 2 the thespians wear smiles?

Natural Selection requires a time lag in order to get results from its non-thinking sorting process. Conscious selection requires a time lag to see what reality produces. Life is an experiment. Is it worth living? Ask a fern. Ask a cat. If you ask a human sometimes you will get an answer. What if you asked all 6.5 billion humans on planet earth?

There came a time in my life when I had to ask myself the toughest questions that I could think of. I played the subject/object game. The questioning came as a result of a lengthy "Dark Night of the Soul." What is life? What am I doing here? Where did I come from? Where am I going? Do I have any control over it? How should I live my life? Out of depression and despair a new life can be born. Has any other human ever gone through this? Lots of them have. St. John of the Cross, a 16th Century Spanish Monk, coined the phrase "The Dark Night of the Soul." St. John wrote a book about it. In his book he said that he took consolation out of the sufferings of those from the past who wrote about it. One was David who St. John found in the Psalms. A book within the Septuagint. The Psalms are ancient Hebrew writings from the "hearts" of real people. Guess what? They had plenty of "Dark Nights."

St. John alludes to David's Psalm 62. My Old Testament had it in Psalm 63. "O God you are my God; Early will I seek You; My flesh longs for You. In a dry and thirsty land where there is no water (St. John's OT called it the "desert"). So I have looked for You in the sanctuary, to see Your power and Your glory." The land of metaphors and the mystical have swung open their gates to the soul wandering in the Dark Night. David was looking for an "energy field" that would get him out of the desert. In Psalm 38 David says, "I am troubled, I am bowed down greatly; I go mourning all the day long. For my loins are full of inflammation, and there is no soundness in my flesh. I am feeble and severely broken; I groan because of the turmoil of my heart." Later at the end of this particular Psalm David says, "...I follow what is good. Do not forsake me, O Lord; O my God, be not far from me! Make haste to help me, O Lord, my salvation." St. John of the Cross says, "God leads into the dark night those whom He desires to purify from all these imperfections so that He may bring them farther onward."

The mystical is not to be feared. It can be used or abused. Our local star, the Sun, keeps pouring energy to Planet Earth. It is the energy that replaces the energy we have used up. If it were not for the Sun we would not be here. But its immense power can kill us, too. We now become the mediator. We choose the power for life or death.

Science relies on what is testable and repeatable. Scientists experiment to find what works and what doesn't. In the world of the human psyche repeatability is hard to come by. That is because the experiment, the experimenter and the drama are interconnected. Control groups are hard to control. Things are not as precise as they are in lab tests on the force of gravity. That's why my friend Dr. Feynman referred to psychoanalysis as "witch doctoring."

Early on I knew that I was in the Dark Night. That was an advantage, now that I look back upon the trials that somehow I got through but would not want to live over again. I do remember that my first reaction to the malaise was Deep Prayer. It came naturally. I did it when I was all alone in my secret place. On my stretched out hands and knees I humbled myself before the Universe. Tears flowed from my eyes until I could cry no more. Groans came from my very being. It was OK. It was just God and me. This did not just happen once. It happened often. I did have to get up regularly from those prayers and go out in to the world to make a living. There were many who depended upon me.

Introduction

A recurring phenomenon was that every time I thought things were going to get better they didn't. They got worse. It seemed as if I was always testing bottom or bouncing off bottom as I moved along. It was consolation that many other humans had gone through the same corridor and somehow made it out. But I was also aware of the fact that it was not a sure thing. Just think of all the people on Planet Earth that have perished while still in the dark night. In Deep Prayer I never once put the blame on anybody outside of myself. I thought of the intense despair and depression as a "wake up call" for me. I did ask God for help. The help that I asked for was the help to find problems within me. Were there things lodged so deep in the recesses of my mind that they acted as blocks to progress? "Do the thing you fear the most and the death of fear is certain." Someone famous had said that. I didn't remember who. It sounded timely for me. God if you're going to kill me let's get it over with. I dredged up as much as I could and dealt with it. Still the night wore on.

Reading books became almost an obsession. These were not withdrawal type books. Physics, cosmology, particle physics and astronomy had always had a "mystical" tinge to me. When curious human beings are presented with a mystery, they long to figure it out. I read more books about evolution than you can shake a stick at. If I'm not mistaken Scientific American, in a feature article, named Charles Darwin as the most influential scientist over the last millennium. A vast array of books on human psychology was ingested. Dr. Viktor Frankl's dark night of Nazi concentration camps was read and re-read. Buckminster Fuller, William James and Dr. Emmit Fox became friends across time and space. Carl Sagan's books were re-read. New ones were read. I took particular delight in his "Shadows of Forgotten Ancestors." Carl the cosmologist and Carl the biologist was a fascinating man. He was a "spiritual" man by his own definition, not someone else's.

The Story of the Savior, Jesus of Nazareth

"Complementarity" became real to me. I believe that we not only live in the time lag worlds of classical and quantum physics but in a non-local universe where happenings happen in "no time" or simultaneously. Now that is mystical.

My meditational times were while doing something mechanical and routine in nature. While running on a safe pathway I would zone out. While doing aerobic exercise at the Y, I would zone out. My lawn took two hours to mow. I would try to bring my mind to blankness. Clear out as much "garble" as I could.

I continued my service to non-profits. There is something about working for others without pay or any hope of self-aggrandizement that is good for the health of the self. The Self cannot be totally selfless, since "individuation" of the human spirit, ego and soul is our greatest gift, at least to me. Bringing the three into balance is the thing. The Tao.

I studied eastern religion and spirituality. Religion and spirituality are two different things. Institutionalized religion invariably corrupts the spiritual core of the "fields" produced by spiritual masters. The masters seek to teach and lead the people to community. The master may have more talent than the student, but is no better than the student. Spirituality is more egalitarian and non-exclusive. It is Universal. The recurring "emperor types" sought to use religion to achieve "unity." Unity emperor style, that is. The saviors, prophets, and sages sought the idea of "community." Diversity and tolerance were imbued into the idea of "community." This was a more horizontal approach. Unity, on the contrary, tended to be vertical. Unity was "deterministic" whereas community came from "freewill." Two words so close, yet so far apart.

Buddha came down from Heaven with his laws. They are not his. He brings them from a higher place. The Institution subtly changes the idea of community into unity by hierarchy. The spiritual becomes exclusive to the "tribe" and is transformed to religion. It becomes "my religion vs. your religion."

Introduction

The ones who interpret the religion to the people are the higher-ups in the hierarchy. They have a vested interest.

Since from 5 years old I was raised in the Protestant Church, I decided that if my "faith" was any good now was the time to find out. Playing the subject/object role I said to myself, "Let's find out as much as we can about western religion. Let's go right to its roots." It's similar to how I challenge myself in Deep Prayer. Go to the roots of your psyche. Maybe there is something there that needs addressing that has been submerged forever and is blocking the flow of blood or energy.

Bucky Fuller taught me to be a self-taught skeptic. Verify for yourself the truth of a claim or a prospective course of action. In Bucky's dark night, just before he was about to take a life-ending dip in Lake Michigan, an apparition appeared to him that gave him one more chance. But he was to be the guinea pig, not someone else. Don't accept hand me down faith. Real faith is real. Real to you. So I combed through the roots of western religion. I didn't just take somebody's words for my faith.

Then I stood over Thomas Jefferson's grave at Monticello. Not right directly over, because there is a fence separating the public from the family graveyard. I was a matter of a few feet away. The crowds had dispersed. I was there all alone. He was known as T.J. to his little community here at self-sustained Monticello. When they were entertaining dignitaries for formal dinners, then they referred to him as Mr. Jefferson. T.J. was a man of the arts; he was somewhat of an intellectual although he worked and lived with the people and they didn't think of him that way. He was an intensely curious man. He was a prodigious writer. While times were good, he made a lot of money - or lets say he had money at his disposal. But he spent it all on his friends who came from all walks of life. He loved people, not things. The first thing one saw when entering through the main door at the home was a huge painting of George Washington. He and T.J. were Freemasons. When

The Story of the Savior, Jesus of Nazareth

Harry Truman redid the White House in the early 1950's, all kinds of Freemason signs and symbols were found painted on the White House walls. Sayings that reeked of the spirit of liberty. Liberty almost defies definition. It is something that is felt as well as defined.

Thomas Jefferson died a poor man. Congress bailed him out by buying the Jefferson Library. We live by ideas. T.J. had ideas that were way beyond the circumstances that he found himself in. He was not a perfect man, but many of his ideas were brought down from Heaven. They are from the Universe that has stages bigger than the one upon which we play. The Revolutionary War was indeed a dark night. Out of it came the Declaration of Independence and the Constitution. They speak to the human dilemma. They are mystical contracts that do their best to instruct mankind as to the Way. They are not perfect because, although brought down from Heaven, they were written by human hands. We, the mediators of today, have been handed the torch of responsibility.

T.J. was bold and brave enough to write his own version of the Bible. The "Jefferson Bible" it is called. Jesus, I am convinced, was Jefferson's number one hero. Not a bad choice. T.J. did allow as how Jesus' work was incomplete. He was crucified, you know, by King George III. T.J. excised much of the "hand-me-down" Bible, as he knew that it was written by inferior minds. Those minds that would dominate rather than enlighten. Jefferson was a man of science. It was part of his pragmatic world. Jefferson's greatest contribution to mankind came through the metaphysical side of him. The mystical side of him. He seemed to be able to access a higher level.

As my response to the dark night wore on I began having dreams. I had always been a dreamer. One who remembers his dreams. Some of these dreams are what Carl Jung would call Big Dreams. There are dreams and then there are Big Dreams. I, now the guinea pig, read as much as I could dig up about paradoxical sleep. You are partially paralyzed while

Introduction

dreaming. In a world full of predators you might not think being paralyzed while asleep would yield fitness. That is why Michel Jauvet referred to it as "paradoxical sleep." We all do it, so there must be something about it that lends survival value to our evolved selves.

At least in part, I told the story of savants to illustrate the immense capability of the human brain. I'll bet it can do tricks that you have never dreamed of. Even though the savant can recite 7600 books by memory, he doesn't know what any of those books mean. Meaning is more of a feeling of what you have read or experienced. The part of the savant's brain that has to do with finding meaning in what it takes in was damaged. What if through the way we live we could exercise our brains? I know that I think of my brain as a muscle as well as a computer.

I will share my big dreams with you. Then you must know that I started popping up wide-awake in the middle of the night with answers to my many questions dancing in my head. I must write them down, I thought. I can straighten them out later. I do have a stack of legal paper that contains 1500 pages that I call "garble." I would ask my brain to solve a problem or conundrum for me. If I also cooperated by packing it with as much knowledge as I could on a particular subject and left it alone for a while, my brain would sort it for me. I was always careful to study all sides of an issue. There may be more than two sides. Out of a much larger stack that was constantly kneaded like bread dough, came three stories about how the New Testament was written. I would look at the Bible that I had spent 50 some years reading, partially memorizing, and being told what something or other meant, and in sudden flashes and epiphanies could clearly see its structure. It's scaffolding, if you will. "Where did this come from?" I thought. Had I accessed Akashic records or Jung's Collective Unconscious? What strange things had the atoms in my brain coughed up? Maybe if you seek hard enough you will find.

The Story of the Savior, Jesus of Nazareth

    The first story of this "trilogy" is about the Savior, Jesus of Nazareth. The second story is about a transformed man, one Saul of Tarsus, who became an Apostle. He invented the word Apostle to describe himself. He was the one to call Jesus of Nazareth Crist (Greek for Christ). Paul, the new man, became a revolutionary against Roman authority, just as Jesus had been. The ones who followed Paul were convinced that Jesus was returning any minute. They were the martyrs who gave their lives for a cause. They have yet to be honored. They were not honored in the New Testament because the New Testament was the work of a powerful Roman Emperor. He reached a quid pro quo with many off-shoots of the original revolution led by Jesus of Nazareth. A state religion was the baby conceived of by Constantine the Great. Constantine and the Council of Nicaea is the third story of the trilogy. I call it the "Libera me, Domine ('Liberate Me, Lord') Trilogy." The state religion, geared for the 4th Century AD, still is in existence today - 1600+ years later. This state religion spawned the myriad of Protestant churches that we see today. They are not the religion of Jesus of Nazareth but of a Roman Emperor.

    First, I will tell you four of the dreams. Then I will tell you the first story. The Story of the Savior, Jesus of Nazareth. Get ready for an Odyssey of the Mind.

Part II

The Dreams

Dream One
The House Dream

The Dream occurred first in my Dark Night of the Soul.

The dreamer is standing on the public walking sidewalk facing a 1950'ish white two-story house. It's a balmy summer day. The dreamer notices the front lawn on either side of the sidewalk to the house. The lawn looks neat and freshly mowed; the grass is green. There is an oak tree growing on the left side of the lawn. The hedges in front of the house on both sides of the front door are symmetrical and appear to have been freshly clipped. A two-car attached garage is to the right of the house and indented a few yards from the front of the house. The garage door is closed.

The dreamer walks towards the house on the private sidewalk and walks up two steps on the brick stairs to the front door. The dreamer does not ring the front bell or knock, but opens the door and walks right in. To the dreamer's right is the living room. There is an airy, open feeling. There is no one home. The dreamer feels comfortable. To the left is the dining room. Further past the living room to the right is the entranceway to the kitchen; this area is also maybe a kind of den area. Everything is very well lighted; not with artificial light, but from natural light. The décor of the house is light, too.

Now the dreamer notices a few steps straight ahead of him a stairway leading to the second floor. On the right side of the stairway is a railing with a solid oak cap. It appears to have been cleaned and polished recently. The stairway is carpeted. The carpeting is grey and plush. As the dreamer climbs the stairway, he feels the plushness of the carpet under his feet - he reaches the top.

The Story of the Savior, Jesus of Nazareth

The dreamer now is standing at the second floor landing. To his left is a doorway. The door is closed. Ahead lays the hallway to other rooms on the second floor. The dreamer now turns and faces the door. There is the doorknob. Now he feels concern. Should he open the door? Might there not be something behind that door that he shouldn't see or perhaps, doesn't want to see? Maybe he should continue down the hallway. Other rooms might have open doors where he can see what's inside before entering. No he cannot do this, something strong inside him is urging or pushing him to open the door. He reaches out to the doorknob, first tentatively and then purposefully grasps the knob, turns it to the right and ... opens the door. He looks in. The room is small almost closet like, but it is windowed top to bottom with three windows; they are latticework windows with several small, clear glass window panes. The room is empty; the carpeting is plush and the same color as the carpeting on the stairway and the second floor hallway. The room is clean and smells good and well ventilated, not musty like you might expect from a room whose door had been closed for a while. But the most predominant visual features were the sunbeams coming in through the lattice glass panes. Much as you can see sunbeams coming through gaps in giant cumulus cloud formations on a warm July day. They were streaming down at a forty-five degree angle and would seemingly vary in intensity as the dreamer luxuriated in their illumination. The dreamer felt warm and good and unafraid as the dream closed.

Dream Two
The Jesus Dream

This Dream occurred second
somewhere in The Dark Night,
I know not when.

The dreamer sees a long, light oak-colored table ahead of him. It is as if he is seeing from about one-fourth of the way down from the top of the table to the three-fourths of the tabletop that is left. At the right corner of the table he sees sitting, himself. (This is the left corner from the dreamer's eyes.) It is as if it is an extension of him. He is at once the dreamer and a participant in the dream, able to see through both sets of eyes. The dreamer sees someone sitting at the other corner opposite and looking at the dreamer's extension of himself.

The room is well lit; in fact there might be a lit, single white candle in a cooper saucer dish candleholder on the table. The flame is flickering. "Oh my God!" thinks the dreamer - the other person is Jesus! He is smiling and looking toward the other corner at the dreamer's extension of himself. Now the dreamer sees through two sets of eyes, the dreamer's eyes and the extension's eyes. The dreamer's extension is smiling too. At the same time the dreamer sees his extension and Jesus they rise to a standing position. The extension sees the same, but from its own viewpoint.

Jesus is wearing a white tunic with short sleeves (his summer attire). The tunic stops three-fourths the way down his thighs and has a black tie-band around the waist. He is wearing laced sandals on his feet, tied around his ankles and lower legs. His legs are slightly hairy with black hair. He has a half-

The Story of the Savior, Jesus of Nazareth

cropped black beard, black mustache, and black well-kept thick hair over his ears and about half way down his neck. The hair is somewhat curly. The hair in front is brushed up and back so that his forehead is exposed. The eyes are sparkling. The dreamer notes that he looks almost like a marathon runner (probably from all that walking he does, thinks the dreamer). But the dreamer is a little surprised at what Jesus looks like. He looks Roman or Greek.

Now they approach each other - the dreamer and his extension both notice that Jesus is smiling and is in a light mood as they approach. The dreamer notices that his extension is smiling too. Then Jesus and the dreamer's extension meet and both reach out their arms to one another and embrace, both still smiling, so happy are they to see one another. It is as if they are best of friends and know each other well. Both are firm huggers. Then Jesus pulls his shoulders back somewhat; his right hand grasping my extension's left shoulder and his left hand grasping my right shoulder. My right hand doesn't quite reach his left shoulder, but clasps his left upper arm. The dreamer now sees his face again. He looks different; he wears a robe, not a tunic. The robe goes down to his ankles. His hair now is more brownish than black. He has a beard and mustache but brownish like his hair; his hair is longer now too. His face is different - it is more what I expected him to look like, I think to my dreamer self. He looks more, well, Jewish - less modern. Very handsome. The most striking thing is that he's having a big laugh right in front of me, still clasping my shoulders and even patting them as he continues to guffaw. The dream fades out.

Dream Three
The Mountain Dream

This Dream helped me endure the Dark Night.
There were others almost as big, but not quite.

My friend and I are in a car, maybe an early 50's car and we are in say, Colorado. It's a beautiful, balmy, summer day and we have the windows rolled down and our arms out the windows. Puffy cumulus clouds drift overhead and are contrasted with the deep blue of the sky. We are driving up a mountain, up a mountain pass.

Suddenly, we reach a fog; this is what in the winter we would call a "whiteout." Behind us it's clear, in front you can't see anything. We see a couple of cars that left the road and are abandoned. One is a station wagon (I think a mid-70's Pontiac station wagon.)

We both get out of the car. My friend thinks we should look around for some other people to see if there's anything they know about this situation. He suggests we split up and start looking down where it's still clear. My friend stays where it's clear and safe.

Without even thinking, I head into the fog or whiteout. It's still warm. I am walking up now, like walking up a ski slope. I can't see anything, but know I'm going up. At some point I reach a place where the slope appears to be very steeply inclined, and in reaching out my foot I'm also trying to figure out how I'm going to make it up this steep slope.

I look up and the fog is beginning to break up. I see patches of blue overhead, and at the top of the slope I see a scrubby bush or tree. This is a tree I've seen before; it grows at very high altitudes and lives to be very old. This tree is actu-

The Story of the Savior, Jesus of Nazareth

ally within arm's reach and could be used to pull myself up this severe slope.

As I reach out I realize that the tree may be my only choice. I also am afraid that the tree, because it looks so beaten (no leaves, gnarled limbs), is actually dead and when I grab it, it will break and I will tumble backwards.

I grab the nearest limb and it is strong - it is alive! I pull myself up and over the slope. The fog is now behind me and I have a sense of being up and over the top. I go onward, now down somewhat, onto a ledge. I am not frightened at being on this ledge. There is no one else here. The sky is again a beautiful blue. There are no clouds.

I am now looking out over a beautiful lush valley that stretches to the horizon. I see the road that my friend and I had been on. It goes down the mountain, through the valley, and starts to rise somewhat as it meets the horizon. I am filled with awe and feel warm and good.

Again, without thinking, I turn around; I must go back for my friend. I go back through the fog and back down to the place where we had left the car. My friend is not there. I go into the woods and head in the direction he was going the last time I saw him. I come upon a log ski lodge. It looks quite cozy. I go in. It's rustic and there is a fire crackling in the fireplace. The proprietor appears. He is in Lederhosen and looks quite Austrian. He's not fat, but husky. Lots of good German beer, Schnitzels. He asks if he can help me. I want to know if he has seen my friend. Just as the proprietor is about to speak, my friend appears. I look at him, and he looks at me. I say to him "I have found the way." He looks at me warmly and motions with a nod of his head, which I take to mean, "let's go." And we leave together.

Dream Four
The Oak Tree Dream

This Dream gave me the final approval that I needed.

Somewhere in space and time I had a dream. It occurred sometime in or around my "Dark Night of the Soul." The "Dark Night" is a metaphysical plane of existence that many human beings enter. Some, having entered, never make it out; some do and are changed by the experience. Those that make it to the dawn sometimes feel compelled to share the experience with the world. Perhaps another voyager may like to know that there is the dawning of the light, and that the experience, which at the time may seem overwhelming, may transform your life. Transform your life for the better.

At once I am the dreamer, the lead actor (the only actor), and the observer. The action takes place in my backyard. I laid the sod in most of the backyard in the early 1960's. It is my personal zoo. A creek runs through it. We are at a bend in that creek. The water molecules find their way to the Mississippi River, then cascade downstream to a river delta in Louisiana where they become part of an ocean. It looks like a good trout stream, but it isn't. I've had hundreds of "water" dreams - however, this one wasn't about water; it was about Oak Trees. We have one Red Oak and several White Oaks. They produce fruit, the acorn. The fruit is enjoyed by ducks, squirrels, and deer, just to name a few. Chipmunks seem to like acorns. They breed in numbers but are suckers to fox. A fox will sit at a woodpile, with ears perked, just waiting for a chunky little acorn-fed chipmunk to make his appearance. Sometimes it appears. Sometimes it has gone down a hole and resurfaced at another location where no fox awaits. Chipmunks can't see very well, but they are good at making more chipmunks.

The Story of the Savior, Jesus of Nazareth

Most White Oaks in our backyard are mature and are probably seventy-five feet tall. We have a hill in the backyard that kids slide down all winter long. The creek has gouged out a little valley over thousands of years. The house sits up top, of course, and we have never had a problem with flooding. The deer will come right up on our back patio for corn, bird seed, or an occasional apple. The animals in our neighborhood are all well fed. The suburban governments all say, "don't feed the animals," but the problem persists. People like me just love having their own zoo.

The actor in the dream is me. He wanders through "his" backyard checking out its condition. Lo and behold one of the giant oaks has a huge chunk loose near the base. If the chunk came loose the tree would surely fall. Is this safe with all the kids in the neighborhood, including my two grandchildren, down there all the time? I ask the rhetorical question. With liberation comes responsibility. I must solve the problem now. If I pull the chunk out, will the oak's submission to gravity take me down with it? Let's see now - if I move it this way, it does not appear that it will. I make my move. The tree responds to gravity and falls away from me. It has not damaged any other trees either. It was a soft landing.

The feeling is one of warmth. The oak's time was now. It will be sawed into chunks that will make another nice woodpile for the animals.

If one acts upon one's dreams they are predictive of the future. Like Odysseus, I headed out into the unknown. My dreams can be played back in my mind's "eye" any old time. How do our dreams affect the world of reality? We shall see.

Thinking About the Dreams

Dr. Carl Jung, who analyzed some 50,000 dreams in his lifetime, said (paraphrasing the Dr.) that the student should learn everything he can about why we dream and the "meaning" of the dreams, and then forget about what he has learned and go for it. Ultimately, it is not Dr. Jung who knows the dreamer's dream, but the dreamer.

My dreams were about Evolution, Change, or Process. Relativity Theory stops the "fundamentalist" physicist dead cold in his tracks. He has a hard time with quantum physics or the quantum mechanics. It was hard enough absorbing Relativity. Now comes a new theory. The "fundamentalist" of religion has a hard time in the same way. New theories that clash with something 1400 or 1675 or 2200 or 2500 years old are heresy. My dreams beckoned me to become a new person. The same me yet a new me. The old me didn't go away. He changed. Ice changes to water at 32 degrees Fahrenheit. At 212 degrees, it changes to steam and rises to Heaven, only to be metamorphosed again into the rain that brings new life to a parched desert. The thermodynamics of reality.

My dreams motivated me to use all the mental skills I could muster to confront the roots of a "faith" that was handed down to me, as it is to millions of people. The dreams convinced me to take a journey of discovery, or an odyssey of the mind, if you will. If there was something there, then I would confirm what had been fed into my brain by my environment. If not, I would not have to have second thoughts on my deathbed. I was honoring free will the only way that I could. Use it or lose it. God's most precious gift. If, perchance, I found some pearl on this odyssey, I would share it with the world.

In the dreams the Self and self, the Spirit and the ego,

become whole. They are partners in the creative process of building the Self. Creation didn't "happen." Creation is "happening."

Let me illustrate in another way. Universe itself has evolved and is evolving every second. From our perspective riding on the Pale Blue Planet, we see:

1.) Inorganic evolution by gravitational selection—gravity sorts the outwardly expanding stuff into stars, groups of stars, galaxies, groups of galaxies, and then groups of groups of galaxies;
2.) Organic evolution through natural selection and major change events;
3.) Organic evolution through conscious selection.

The three main categories listed above are merely the high points. It in reality is a continuum that is moving. Each category could be subdivided as much as you'd like. For example, one could talk about the creation and evolution of the elements, and then the creation and evolution of chemical compounds. Further, there probably are higher levels that either haven't happened or of which we are not aware. "Levels" and "Fields" and our singular and communal awareness of them are part of the tapestry of Universe.

Organic evolution cannot do away with what came before. It is built upon what came before. It adds a new layer of "complexity" to the past, its creator. Conscious Selection then builds upon its "Creator." "Social Contrivances" are created by human minds, as organic "phenotypes" are created by genes. Phenotypes are engaged in a selective process that some refer to as "survival of the fittest." Social Contrivances created by human minds are engaged in a selective process. Governments, laws, economic systems, political parties, religions, and corporations are the ideas brewed up in the minds of Homo sapiens. Your minds, in a sense, are the genes of social structures. The

Thinking About the Dreams

naturally selected have no "Mediator." It is a snapshot of one infinitesimal moment in time of what organisms are left standing. They are the fittest. They may not be tomorrow. Cultural selection can be conscious. The selection of Social Contrivances is both natural and conscious. "Hey! This isn't working." "Yeah? Says who?" Some people blindly follow what has been told them. Some people don't. Free will could be the greatest gift of the evolving Universe to itself.

The story you are about to read is mystical. It is spiritual. It is about a man who talked about the "Son of Man" and who was an example of that being. Universe is building levels of itself. New levels transcend but do not do away with the old level. This man talked of salvation. If we believe him we can "Ascend." We can build new levels of cultural complexity that serve mankind and make life happier and more meaningful for everyone. Humans can't fly like a bird. They can fly better than a bird.

Part III

The Story of the Savior, Jesus of Nazareth

Rubens - The Meeting of Abraham and Melchizedek
According to Genesis 14:17-21, this meeting actually took place between Abram and Melchizedek; Abraham was the name he was later known by.

The Lord said to my Lord,
Sit at my right hand,
'Till I make your enemies your footstool.
The Lord shall send the rod of your strength out of Zion,
Rule in the midst of your enemies.

Your people will be volunteers
In the day of your power;
In the beauties of holiness,
From the womb of the morning,
You have the dew of your youth,
The Lord has sworn and will not relent,
You are a priest forever
According to the order of Melchizedek.

Psalm 110
The Bible: The New King James Edition

Chapter One
I Must Leave

Nazareth in Palestine, a protectorate of
the Roman Empire, 12 a.d.

"Mother! Mother! Please, I must talk to you now." The handsome fifteen-year-old burst through the door of their smallish, square frame and dried mud home in Nazareth. "Mother" was mending the clothes of her husband Joseph and the four boys. The oldest, Jesus, had not been getting along with the father for quite some time. The other three, ages nine through thirteen, did what they were told to do, which was to work for the father until he said they could do something else.

His mother, Mary, held him in her arms as she would all the boys, playing favorites to none. But this first born was different. Not the typical first born, who fell in line with the family plan and dominated the siblings. Not so with this one. His curiosity was immense. She knew it. The father, Joseph, fought it. They were poor Jewish peasants, he told the boys. We are born to be the workers of society. He showed them a colony of ants. The worker ants were like little well trained slaves. Back and forth they would go doing incredible physical feats to insure the survival of the colony. The only thing the father knew was how to build and repair dwellings. He would labor in the hot sun for hours and hours. Building, building, building. When a project was completed he would build the next one. How long could he go without water or food? He would come home exhausted. Mary would always have food ready for he and the boys. On Saturday, the last day of the week, they rested. The only reason Joseph rested was because he was told to. It was a sin if he did not rest on Saturday.

"Jesus, your father is a hard working man. He appreciates what he has here. He has not been to war to stand on the frontline with a shield. We have food and we are warm. One day per week we rest.

None of our children have died. They are all able to work for the family. No one bursts through our door to see if we hide revolutionaries. He thinks we are very lucky to have what we do. We say thank you to Jaweh for these blessings. Here I have repaired your sandals for you."

"Mother, the Romans that we work for pay us next to nothing. You should see the size of their dwellings. Their colony is only two miles from Nazareth, yet it is like two different worlds. They lounge around taking dips in their pools. They have slaves fanning them with ostrich feathers, as we toil in the hot sun."

"Jesus, be thankful that you are not a slave. You get to come home. The slaves are nothing but property to the Romans. They do all the work while the Romans take boat trips across the Great Sea to Rome, and then come back with the latest in Roman culture. Slaves oar the boats for days, while the Romans eat grapes and fish for delicacies to be cooked while on the trip. They swim in the clear blue waters of the Great Sea while the slaves labor. They have learned how to keep the slaves as physically fit as they can, while their minds have been trained to be numb. Many male slaves are neutered to keep their passions low. Other male slaves are reproducers, but are not allowed to keep their own children. The children are property of the Roman Empire, and the individual slave masters who own them can buy and sell them like donkeys and goats. Just be thankful to Jaweh that you are not one of them Jesus. You come home to me."

"I am thankful mother, but why do these few get to rule over the many? The ones I have talked to don't seem that much

I Must Leave

more intelligent, but there is this barrier where they treat me as if I am an animal. Who gives them that right, Mother? Father doesn't even question it. He works so he doesn't have to even think about it."

"It has always been this way Jesus. It's not for us to question Jaweh. If this wasn't right he would do something about it. He hasn't, so it must be right."

"Mother, I love you, but all these things are welling up inside me that I cannot deny. I cannot work with father any longer. He will be looking for me. I must leave now."

Mary was sobbing, but she understood deep within somewhere. Now was her moment of destiny, and she did not let it pass. "Jesus, I must now tell you something that I did not withhold from you on purpose. It had to be the right time. Joseph is not your father, but he took me in when I was at the depths of my despair. I was deeply in love as a young girl with a handsome, compassionate Arab who had come here with a caravan from far to the east. He had the most beautiful olive skin, just like you. I was pregnant with you and we were to be married. I would have gone anywhere with him. One day the Roman soldiers took him away from Nazareth with several other young men. They were tied together and led off by the soldiers on horses. I never saw him again." She was sobbing as Jesus held her in his strong arms. "Mother, if it's the last thing I do, I will vindicate you and my father. I must know why this is. It is not right. I must leave. I cannot lead my life this way."

"Jaweh be with you my beloved son. We will make it. I can handle your father; he has three other sons who are not like you. Will I ever see you again?"

"I keep your image in my mind. I can call it up when I need to. I can feel your warmth. I can even smell you. You will be with me always. I will return if I can."

"Go then Jesus, I will not prevent you from being what you must be. Let me fix a pack for you with goods to keep you for a week."

The Story of the Savior, Jesus of Nazareth

Jesus knew exactly where he was going. In the little time he had to himself on Saturdays he was not playing games like the other youngsters. He liked girls but, he had a compulsion within him that allowed him to not have to think about young ladies all of the time, like his peers. He did not condemn them for that. He felt the urges but they would have to take second place for a while. There was something in him that riled him about the Roman snobs who thought they were better than anyone else. Why was this? He saw the Pharisees bowing down to the Romans. The Sadducees were ambivalent. The young men in the areas around Jerusalem were united by their religion, but they were not united in their hate for the Romans. Some accepted their miserable lives as fate while they watched the Romans, with their servants, slaves, and the latest in clothing, parade themselves as Gods gift to earth. They knew that it was Roman soldiers who allowed them to do what they did. Yes, the people had an underlying fear of reprisal, harsh reprisal, if they did not fall in line with the Roman "system." This underlying fear governed their very lives.

While at the Temple in Jerusalem, which Jesus had visited on certain religious days, he had read the Torah and talked to other young men like himself from other parts of Palestine. He found out that many of them shared his feelings about the Roman occupiers. Some of them talked of older brothers who would not come to the Temple anymore because it was controlled by the Pharisees, who they thought had "sold out" to the Romans. There was a "buzz" in the air amongst these young men. Jesus thought that they were angry. He sensed trouble coming. Some of the young men talked of men who were very smart and just couldn't put up with the Romans or the Pharisees. They had the skills to be self sufficient as a group and were peace-loving men. The Pharisees and the Romans wanted to control them. It was impossible for them to be controlled. But they didn't want to start a war. They formed a "secret" community called Qumran about forty miles from Jerusalem.

I Must Leave

A self-sustaining community where they were "free." They had been there for sometime. Most of the other young men just swallowed their pride and continued on. Jesus was sure that's what his three brothers would do.

There were other signs that Jesus saw. Most men in Jewish society, when not working, were drinking lots of wine. Jesus had tried it and found that, to a certain point, wine would give one a sense of relief from the pain of day to day existence. But most men used it to inebriate themselves, permanently withdrawing from reality's harshness. It had its bad side. Some drunks became dangerous. Others became morose, losing interest in life because they couldn't handle the pain. And with good reason, Jesus thought. Was this their fault or society's fault? What was society anyway? How come life was so hard? He had never gotten to know his real father because the Romans took him. The rabbis read, staccato style, from the Torah with heads down. Some would read for hours. They observed the oldest rituals.

The rabbi defined what sin was. If you tied a rope a certain way on Saturday, it was a sin because you were "working." If you tied it another way, you were not sinning. People lined up at the rear of the Temple with cats and dogs, rabbits, sheep, cows, and old mules. They would transfer their sin to the animal. The priest would take the animals and sacrifice them on an altar as "payment" to Jaweh. Jesus had read the story of Abraham in the Torah. He would have sacrificed his son Isaac as propitiation, had not Jaweh intervened and provided a ram as a substitute. Jesus thought that there was at least one intelligent man in the world who had the courage to change a stupid tradition of sacrificing human male babies to Jaweh. What kind of Jaweh could this be? What was it about killing some living thing that they thought would make Jaweh happy or appeased? Jesus felt good. He was healthy and strong; he loved life. He loved the smells in the air at harvest time. He loved being with his friends and playing games. He enjoyed the

The Story of the Savior, Jesus of Nazareth

company of young ladies. Some of them liked to have "serious" talks. Some of them were more playful.

Things didn't seem right. How could people go from happy, playful, curious children to an adult who was totally different? He saw more sadness than happiness, more bad things happened than good things, and nobody seemed to know what to do about it. Jesus felt as if he had a wonderful life to live. Was sweating twelve hours a day under the sun, building things for the cheap, bastard Romans any way to live? Why wasn't anybody doing something about this? He had to know. He just had to know.

Jesus loved the story of Abram so much that he named his donkey Abe. Abe was short for Abram. "Abe" was older than the hills but could still produce. Jesus was no dummy. What little time he had to himself was spent mostly assuaging his curiosity. Sometimes he would "kill two birds with one stone." A pretty little girl might accompany him on his forays to find out what was over the next hill. On Jewish Holidays he traveled south to Jerusalem. Not everyone had donkeys. A donkey and a cart was a luxury. Only the Romans had Arabian horses. They were sleek and powerful. The best money could buy. Even the Roman children had beautiful Arabian horses. He remembers watching as a spoiled Roman eight-year-old complained when he was told he must take care of the beautiful, goldish-brown mare that he had been given. Jesus was building the stone wall eight feet high around the home in which they lived. The stables were behind the home, administered by slaves. The eight-year-old threw a fit. "I don't want to," he said. The mother gave in, rather than listen to him bitch. The slaves would do it as usual. The father worked for the government in Jerusalem. He would not be back here until time permitted. Jesus would have given his eyeteeth for that horse. Old "Abe" would have to do.

Qumran was not as "secret" as everyone thought. Jesus got there easily by "dead reckoning." The Jordan River, the

I Must Leave

Dead Sea - such a mountaintop! When those two mountains intersect as you are heading Northwest, you will see a group of caves. They are near the entrance to Qumran. "Young man, what are you doing here in this God-forsaken place?"

Jesus: I am here to find James the Righteous.

James: What does he look like?

Jesus: They told me he was an old man but very wise. They said he could be found near these caves, at the small village surrounded by Palms.

James: How old?

Jesus: No one knows for sure. He is so old he doesn't even know.

James: What do you want from him? Are you a Roman tax collector?

Jesus: Would I be riding this old donkey, with little food and little water, and no soldiers to protect me if I was a Roman tax collector?

James: (He smiles) You still didn't answer my question.

Jesus: I am unarmed, I bear no malice. I have heard so many things about him.

James: From who? Where?

Jesus: I've heard when I go to the Temple in Jerusalem.

The Story of the Savior, Jesus of Nazareth

James: Why don't you get down off that old animal and we will sit in the shade and talk?

The sun is setting behind the mountains now and the air is starting to cool down. The two conversationalists sit on a bench, amongst Palm trees, a few hundred yards from some stone and brick dwellings and a wall built about six feet high.

Every once in a while Jesus sees the top of a head moving along. To his right and to the east he sees the Dead Sea. To the left, where the sun starts its descent through the ravines, he sees vertical limestone cliffs, etched over the centuries into artwork. Artwork created by the water and wind's relentless obedience to their laws of interaction.

Jesus: I have come to learn as much as I can.

James: Why, you can do that back at the Temple in Jerusalem!

Jesus: No I can't. The teachers have sold out to the Romans. Their brains are numbed. All they do is mumble repetitive prayers with heads down. Life is over for them, but they have years before they will die. They say that here there are still some learned people - and no Romans.

James: What makes you think the Romans won't come here young man? If you found us, the Romans surely can.

Jesus: You do not have money in your village. You do not own very much. They say women aren't allowed here. You are passive and won't fight. The Romans really have nothing to come here for. You don't have crops. The limestone cliffs don't hold gold and silver.

James: Are we also stupid?

I Must Leave

Jesus: That's what I want to find out. The smartest ones I know say that the really smart ones live here.

James: Why would they? After what you've said it sounds like an awful place to me.

Jesus: Not if it doesn't attract the Romans. I detest those snobs. I work for my father for twelve hours a day, six days a week to build their homes while they bask in the sun and play. They make me sick. I couldn't take it anymore. My father is numbed to them. All he does is work. That way he doesn't have to think about his miserable life. I finally ran away from him. Then my mother tells me he isn't my real father; I am confused. I have to know why things are like this.

James: Come with me my young friend, I will introduce you to him.

Chapter Two
Qumran

Jesus has Abe's tether and they walk together towards the entrance to Qumran - a fascinating journey for a fifteen-year-old from Nazareth. It would be a journey that would change the world. As they near the gate to the village, Abe and Jesus are startled by a young man in a tunic, who has hopped upon the wall and looks down at the threesome only a few feet from the gate. James looks up.

Young man (with a big grin): James, what have you got there, a young Roman soldier on leave looking for sex and wine? Tell him there are no women here. Tell him he can't get drunk here. Tell him we have no money. If he doesn't leave, strangle him.

Jesus is bewildered, so is Abe.

James: Get down from there, Michael, and help me. This is my new friend from Jerusalem.

Jesus: Not Jerusalem, Nazareth.

Michael: What's his name? Does he have a name?

James: Yes, it's Jesus.

Michael (hopping down, approaches with a grin and hugs Jesus): If James says you're a friend, then you are a friend of mine too.

Qumran

Jesus smiles. Abe snorts. Michael takes the reins of Abe.

Michael: I will bring this interesting animal to the stables. He won't bite me will he?

Jesus: Do you have any dates?

Michael: I have two left in my pocket

Jesus: Why don't you give him one of them and then lead him to water? You and he will be friends forever.

Michael fumbles in his pocket and, sure enough, out comes a date. Abe's lips and the date are one. The two new friends stroll off looking to quench Abe's thirst.

Jesus: So you are "James the Righteous."

James: I am James, some have called me righteous.

Jesus: You don't call yourself righteous?

James: I redefine righteous every day. If there was some way to make it sound not so final, I could accept it.

Jesus: They told me you were old and wise. You look young.

James: I'm thirty-two. That's old. I don't know if I'm wise or not. But let's not stand here. Do you want to enter the village?

Jesus (looking straight ahead at the gate): That's why I came. This gate would not be allowed at the Temple. Only one person can squeeze through it at a time. Can I learn a lot here?

The Story of the Savior, Jesus of Nazareth

James: Do you think that if you learn a lot, things will be easier for you?

Jesus: I don't know, but I have no choice.

James: Yes, you do. Once you pass through this gate your life will change forever. It gets harder not easier. You will learn things you might not like to learn. You can go back now. As bad as the Romans are, you can find a crack to live in. If you're smart enough to find your way here, you're smart enough to find a "living crack."

Jesus: That's not for me. That's no life. I've got to know why things are the way they are, even if it kills me.

James unlatches the gate. Jesus turns sideways and squeezes through.

Jesus (as James slides through): The fat people can't get out of here.

James: The fat people can't get in here.

The two, having made it through, now head for a building larger than a dwelling. James tells Jesus that they head for the "Community Building." Jesus hears a woman's voice.

Voice: James, James where have you been?

James: Anne, this is my new friend Jesus.

She smiles at Jesus. She is a gorgeous Arab girl with olive skin. Her skin is perfect. Her eyes are clear and look right at James' new friend. She reaches out her arms, and her hands are palms open. Jesus reaches her and they clasp hands. Jesus is only fifteen, but he knows a gorgeous woman when he sees one.

Jesus: They said that you have no women here.

James: They also told you I was old. They did tell you how to get here though, so all is not lost.

Anne and James laugh, Jesus grins but seems bewildered.

James: Don't expect to figure this out right away. It may take a while to sink in.

Jesus thinks to himself, "I've never heard of an Arab woman named Anne. Maybe she just looks like an Arab. Jews and Arabs look a lot alike anyway. They just talk different. Some of them look different because of their clothing. Maybe that's it."

The three new friends arrive at the "Community Building." James holds out his right arm at the door, his hands open and with a bowing gesture and with the left arm coming around his midsection it seems to beckon Anne and Jesus to enter.

James: Here, let's sit at this table over here and talk.

A five-year-old child comes running in through another door.

Child: Annie, Annie my dumb brother hit me (he sobs).

Anne (cuddling the little boy): Come now Isaac, why did he hit you?

The Story of the Savior, Jesus of Nazareth

Child: Because he's mean.

Anne: Why don't you two stay here and talk, while I tend to this recurring problem?

Jesus: I don't understand. They told me there were no children here. You didn't produce any because the end of the age is coming soon.

James: Who is "they?"

Jesus: I don't know; everybody I talked to about the Essenes at Qumran.

James: Don't believe everything you hear.

Jesus: Is Anne your wife?

James: What is a wife?

Jesus: What do you mean? My mother is my father's wife.

James: I thought you told me he wasn't your father.

Jesus: Not my real father. You know what I mean.

James: Who is your father?

Jesus: That's what I'm trying to find out. Was that your child?

James: No.

48

Qumran

Jesus: Is Anne his mother?

James: No.

Jesus: Are his father and mother here?

James: No.

Jesus: Where are they, back in Jerusalem?

James: They are dead. Both of them.

Jesus' eyes sag. His head bows a little. He is so sensitive that a tear forms in his eye.

Jesus: I'm sorry.

James: I am too.

Jesus: What will happen to them?

James: We will care for them and teach them.

Jesus: But, they are not yours.

James: Yes they are.

Jesus: Anne looks like she's maybe Arabian.

James: Lucky guess, Jesus. Most people can't tell Jews from Arabs.

Jesus: She's beautiful.

The Story of the Savior, Jesus of Nazareth

James: You have a keen eye. She is even more beautiful on the inside. Her real name is Nura bint Ahmed bin Saleh Al-Fulani. I renamed her for inside our community here.

Jesus: Is James your real name? Are you Hebrew?

James: My given name is Laudabilis.

Jesus: What are names for?

James: You are the curious one. How much time do you have?

Jesus: As much as it takes to learn.

James: All right. Names are symbols. The Hebrews learned this from the ancients.

Jesus: You mean like Abram, Isaac and Jacob, the patriarchs.

James: No, even before them.

Jesus: Who was before them?

James: Melchizedek.

Jesus: Who came before Melchizedek?

James: That's where we stop. Our oldest writings on papyri and copper sheets come down from Melchizedek. He had come from far to the east - at least a one-year journey by horse or camel from here.

Jesus: Why did he come here?

Qumran

James: To escape the warlords. His ancestors in the writings came from somewhere around here. Probably to the north of us. They left there for the same reason and went east.

Jesus: Strange.

James: Not so, when you understand. His ancestors were people of knowledge and builders of society. They built buildings. They were physicians. They came up with ingenious ideas to help one another. They were peaceful and had learned not to pick fights with others not of their same beliefs. However, the warlords changed society by ruling with force. The warlords were more interested in fighting one another. They ruled by coercion. They forced these builders to work for them. Finally, these people, when they had had enough, packed up and left in the middle of the night and headed far to the east. They had enjoyed a great society for about one thousand years. Then the warlords from the east of them came in and took over the society they had so carefully built. They were no good at war - they despised it. The warlords came in with armies that killed as many of the males as they could. They raped the women. A few of Melchizedek's people escaped through a mountain "pass." They journeyed another year to get back here and founded Jerusalem. They originally called it Salem. Abram had come from the north and east of here. He encountered Melchizedek. Melchizedek heard of this huge mass of people emigrating toward the area, because of droughts and disease near the land between the two rivers. Melchizedek had great courage. He rode alone on his horse to meet them. He asked to talk to their leader.

Jesus: This is a fascinating story.

James: It gets more fascinating.

The Story of the Savior, Jesus of Nazareth

James (again): Abram was brought forth. Melchizedek wanted to size up this group without letting them know who he was. He, of course, was non-threatening because he rode in alone and without a weapon. They could have killed him, but for what?

Jesus: How many of them were there?

James: We will never know for sure, Jesus, but there may have been as many as ten thousand people in the huge caravan that stretched for miles. They brought everything with them. They were "tent" people - migrants who moved around depending on what conditions were like.

Jesus: How did they differ from Melchizedek?

James: Melchizedek and his people were artisans. Melchizedek himself was a "stone-mason." He knew how to build permanent structures on good ground that would withstand the elements of nature. They were smart enough to learn how to bring in water from some place else. They stored enough water so that when hard times came, they would not have to expend their energy wandering around looking for it. They stored food. They found ways to preserve food. They built cities. His ancestors had built cities to the north, like Rome, before they ran from the warlords.

Jesus: This reminds me of the story of Joseph in the Torah.

James: Where do you think Joseph learned this? He also learned about the interpretation of dreams from Melchizedek's "Order." His other brothers were out working in the fields for their father Jacob. Joseph, being the smart one, wanted to learn a better way than hard work. Hard work numbs the mind. It makes you dumb. You work repetitiously learning nothing. The father Jacob sat in his tent, while the boys brought him food for himself and his women.

Jesus: And they became jealous of Joseph, didn't they?

James: Yes they did.

James: Melchizedek told Abram that they had started a city not too far east of here called Salem. You know it today as Jerusalem. It had plenty of water and much stored grain. Melchizedek told them that rather than fight with you we would be happy to help you. Come to our city. Look it over. If you want to move on, by all means do so. Abram ended up staying. Melchizedek ended up going back east on a huge trading caravan. So Abram and Melchizedek were together for only a few years. But Abram paid Melchizedek well to learn. A school was set up to teach the artistry of peaceful living. As you might guess, this only lasted so long and the bullies with armaments subjugated them on and off for centuries.

Jesus: How can I learn the artistry of peace making, James? I want to change the world.

James: You are only fifteen-years-old Jesus. You might be biting off more than you can chew.

Jesus: I don't care. Someone has got to do this.

James: If you really, really want to do this, I can teach you. Well, not just me. I can come up with a curriculum that, if followed, by the time you are, say, thirty years old, would prepare you to give something to the world. You can't go running through the streets condemning the Romans. You must be able to show people a better way. Then if they believe in your message you at least will have the Romans outnumbered. It's all about power, Jesus. They rule by force. It works. If you become one of them, you might have a better life. The temptation will be there, believe me. Many who were before you ended up selling their souls for immediate gain. And why not? You must answer this question all the time. Why not? Your power must be greater than theirs.

Jesus: I promise I won't sell my soul James.

James: Promises you make now are next to meaningless. You can argue your way out of any promise you've made. And, in truth, some promises should be broken.

Jesus: How then can I convince you to help me?

James: It is me that must take the chance. I cannot control you. I choose not to control anyone. The freedom inside our minds is the greatest gift we could possibly have. It is the greatest gift you can give to anyone. To help others to free their minds is God's work.

Jesus: But how can I free their minds if their bodies are controlled by the Romans?

James: It's not just the Romans, Jesus. Their minds might be in slavery to sex or money or power. They might be in slavery to work. They might be slaves to things that numb their minds, like wine or smoke from certain plants. They might be slaves to their guilt or a religion that makes them feel guilty. They could be a slave to infirmities of the body or the mind.

Qumran

Jesus: Stop, please stop James! I can't stand it! People don't deserve this lot in life.

James: We will meet again tomorrow and draw up a plan for you. If you decide to take it on, you could change the world. If not, I certainly would not be offended. No one has taken me up on it yet.

Jesus: Meanwhile nothing really changes. It does, but appears in a different form.

James: Changes of the mind are different than changes of nature. Changes of the mind have to come differently.

Jesus: The People need to have hope. The Romans say they are free but they are not. Freedom is a hollow word to the people.

James: Hope is an idea Jesus. Someone must live it out. Someone must show the people how to overcome the world. To do this you must be of another world yet come back to this one of reality. Your temptation, Jesus, as you grow, will be to join up with the Prince of this World.

Jesus: Who is the Prince of the World?

James: He is no one in particular. But he is the one who lords it over the people. He might come from the rich or come from the poor, but he separates himself from the people. He becomes their master. His tools of control are money, armaments, anger, temper, religion, and the worst of all violence. He is willing to use violence against his fellow man to control him.

Jesus: Must I fight this Prince?

The Story of the Savior, Jesus of Nazareth

James: You must fight yourself, to prevent yourself from becoming him or one of his underlings.

Jesus: I could never do that.

James: The power is subtle and seductive. The people buy into his power until he asks so much that they revolt. They then go to another who promises them freedom, but ends up just like the one they just left.

Jesus: Why is this?

James: It has always been this way.

Jesus: I want to change the World, James.

James: Tomorrow morning we will talk about the tools you need to do that. Get some sleep. Dream good dreams. Good night, Jesus.

Chapter Three
The Teacher Must Be Taught

Jesus, the fifteen-year-old, spent a restless night. He is so anxious, yet he is so happy he found James. Such good fortune. But he knows that he never would have found James if he hadn't taken the giant step of leaving his beloved mother. His stepfather he wouldn't miss at all. He longed to know his real father, who still had his mother's heart. Jesus wandered outside his quarters. It was cool and he had his heaviest wool robe on. His mother had made it for him. The earliest rays of sunshine, before the sun, were starting to illuminate part of the eastern horizon. He wandered down the well-worn path where they went to look out over the great valley to the east. Nearing the bluff he saw the outline of a man. He was seated on the ground, legs crossed, and looking straight east as the sun slowly emerged from beneath Earth's rim. His outstretched hands rested palms up, one on each knee. He was accepting graciously the power of the Sun's light. Jesus knew that it was James. He walked slowly and quietly to James side. Nothing was said. James eyes were closed. He would not look straight into the Sun even though the morning's rays were not so harmful. Jesus sat beside James. He struck the same pose palms open. With each tiny inch that the Sun rose Jesus could feel his body warm. His robe warmed. They sat like this until the Sun had ascended well above the distant, eastern horizon. James talked first.

James: Jesus, if you are to teach, you must be taught. Your well must be so deep that those who come to you shall never thirst.

The Story of the Savior, Jesus of Nazareth

Jesus: I am willing, James. I do this freely. I have made up my mind. Someone must do this, James.

James: Jesus, do you believe in the God of Isaiah?

Jesus: What do you mean, James?

James: When you go to the Temple on Saturday, do you listen to the rabbi?

Jesus: Yes, but sometimes he talks so fast that I don't follow him.

James: Does he ever explain to you the difference between the Law and the Prophets? Or the Law, the Prophets, and Writings?

Jesus: He has us memorize passages, but he never explains them to us.

James: What else does he say?

Jesus: First we are to obey, we should not question. Then we should work for the Temple. We should bring our sacrificial animals to the Temple, so that the High Priest can offer them as burnt offerings to God to redeem our sins. We are to tithe to the Temple, or God will not be pleased. Our ancestors Moses and Abraham will not be pleased either.

James: The damn Pharisees and Sadducees have you by the short hairs, Jesus!

Jesus: They do not

The Teacher Must Be Taught

James: We must free your mind, Jesus. As you are within your mind so you are without.

Jesus: Without?

James: Your actions, Jesus! The way you lead your life. Your mannerisms, the way you approach someone, the look on your face. The tone of your voice. What you talk about. How you listen. Some people don't even listen to what you are saying in a conversation. All they are interested in is talking themselves. Most people are interested only in themselves.

Jesus: Isn't that natural?

James: Yes.

James (Again): Let's go back to see if Anne's up. We can drink some coffee and eat some fresh bread and talk.

As they near the community they hear the animals first. Donkeys, goats, horses, chickens. When the wind is from the west they would have smelled the animals before they heard them. There is no wind this morning. They enter through the narrow gate. People are up now. "My brother hit me." James and Jesus hear the familiar lament. They hear Anne's calming voice, "Boys will you please be nice to one another." "He started it," says the older voice. "You liar!" says the younger voice. Anne speaks, "That's enough or you will both be without play time today. You will both have to go gather wood for the fire during playtime." There was silence. Maybe if they were good for a while, she would forget about what she had said.

Jesus: James, I'm very confused about women.

James: Aren't we all?

The Story of the Savior, Jesus of Nazareth

Jesus: No, I mean I love them. I love my mother more than I love myself but I have these feelings when I see these pretty girls. Not like I feel for mother. Different. Like I want them more than as friends.

James: That's the way I feel too and I'm more than twice as old as you.

They near the community hall.

James: Jesus, let's continue this later. Anne will make Turkish coffee. Have you ever tasted tea from India?

Jesus: I've never heard of Turkish coffee or India.

James: You've been too busy working for the Man. You have much to learn. Before you can help others, you must help yourself. We will make your well a deep one, but it will be up to you. Where will you get the motivation?

Jesus: What do you think I'm doing here, James? I want to know where I came from. I have to know, James.

James: You will not like most of what you find. But if you seek it, Jesus, you will find it. You will learn about the Great Way. First you must learn the bare essentials here with us at Qumran.

Jesus: James, how can I thank you? No one talks like this in Jerusalem.

James: You will only thank me with your life.

Jesus: What do you mean?

The Teacher Must Be Taught

James doesn't answer. They enter the building. The scent of freshly baked bread is recognizable. Jesus smells the smoke of burning mesquite. He is curious about some of the other smells. He sees other men the age of James. Even younger. There are very few old men. The people in Jerusalem are very wrong about Qumran. It is not for dropouts. They are out-foxing the Romans, Jesus thinks. These men like James could never take orders from some Roman dunce, with his sharp sword and dull-brained soldiers. Life somehow means much more to them. How do they get away with this? This is for me, Jesus thinks.

James: Levi, come over here and meet someone.

A handsome young man with a chunk of bread in one hand and a cup with something steamy walks toward Jesus and James. He wears a big smile.

Levi: James! Did you finally get someone to help me shovel the manure out of the stables and mix it for use in our gardens?

Jesus laughs. James holds out his arms, as if to embrace Jesus' new friend to be.

James: He's a strong young man and quite willing to help.

Levi: We don't sacrifice animals down here Jesus. They are too valuable. The Levites should sacrifice themselves. The world would be much better off.

They all sit down at a long table. Anne has arrived minus the two little squabblers.

The Story of the Savior, Jesus of Nazareth

Anne: Good morning, savers of the world!

James: Have you any tea or coffee?

Anne: I'll bring some now, with something for you boys to eat.

Levi: I don't know how James deserves such a fine woman, Jesus (Levi winks at Jesus.)

James: She appreciates my finer qualities.

Jesus: I've never even had a girlfriend. Well I don't mean it that way. What I mean is I have friends that are girls but I've never ...

Levi: Never what young man?

Jesus: You know what I mean.

Levi: And it's a good thing. You don't want to be pregnant at your age Jesus.

Jesus: I don't think my mother was too much older when she had me.

Levi: Well, that's your mother. Did your father stay with her?

James: That's a sensitive subject Levi. Jesus' real father was taken away by Roman soldiers.

Levi: The bastards. One thing worse than Levites is Romans. No, I take that back - they're equal, both of the darkness.

The Teacher Must Be Taught

Jesus: Darkness?

James: Jesus, we talk differently around here. We explain things like the world explains them to us. Darkness is at night. The light is gone. We sleep. The predators are up, awake conniving against we who sleep. When it is light we see them for what they are. We outnumber them. We are the sons of light. They are the sons of darkness.

Jesus: I still don't understand.

James: You will.

Anne returns with pitchers that steam and bread that smells so good. Jesus' mouth waters. He is a hungry young man. He is an excited young man. How come he is so lucky as to be here now with these teachers of the world? He remembers how he had risen early every morning and worked and sweated under the sun. Was that sun a good sun like they think? My father wouldn't even look up sometimes. Sweat, work, sweat, work, sweat, work - for what? So that some spoiled Roman kid could complain about a slave not wiping his ass right. The slave would get reprimanded for not wiping his ass right, while the kid was complaining about something else. Meanwhile the father was in Jerusalem with Pilate figuring out how to control the people. Jesus' father had accommodated himself to this brand of Roman "freedom." Look what we have done for you poor, stupid people who are not as good as us. Why didn't Jesus' father do something about this? His father always made excuses. He wouldn't talk about it much. "How lucky you are Jesus to have work to do. They sent my father to the front shield line. I never knew my father. My mother told me he was killed in his first battle. Be thankful for what you have. It was meant to be this way. We can't change the world. Be thankful you're not a neutered slave or put into battle at sixteen

The Story of the Savior, Jesus of Nazareth

years old." Jesus would shrug. He got this or similar every time. Meanwhile he couldn't help but notice what went on in that little Roman enclave. Why don't those rich bastards change the way things are, he thought?

Levi: Anne, you are a good woman. I am currently between women - are you available?

Anne (smiling): Will you take my two young boys? They would love to keep you up all night.

Levi: I think I'll take a cold bath instead.

James laughs and slaps Levi on the back.

James: She's pretty, but not that pretty, right Levi?

Levi: Let's talk about something else.

They all rip off big hunks of bread. They put goat cheese on the bread and are stimulated by the tea and coffee.

James: I have a wonderful idea.

Levi: Oh! Oh! I think I'm leaving.

James: No, Levi, I'm not going to talk you into repairing the north wall all by yourself. This is serious business.

Anne: Serious business, I don't want.

James: No, no - listen to me! This fine young man who wandered in here not too long ago wants to change the world.

The Teacher Must Be Taught

Levi: Teach him how to run a sword through the Roman Prefect in Jerusalem. Right below his chin.

They chuckle.

James: Kill one, you get another one. Maybe worse. I'm serious now. Would you help me sit here this morning and dream up a plan to educate Jesus, so he can be somebody?

Anne: Who will take care of Aaron and Isaac?

James: Can't you get one of the other girls, just for this morning?

Anne: They already have their hands full.

James: Just once?

Anne: All right, I'll ask, but nobody likes to take care of those two little fighters.

Anne leaves for a while to find a friend she can make a trade with.

Levi: James, he must go on a journey east along the Great Way, to learn from the libraries and the teachers of the history of man's battles with himself.

James: Levi, don't get ahead so fast. All in good time. First Jesus should spend two years here learning a trade, so that he will be useful to society wherever he goes. He can earn and learn. There is no other way to do it.

Levi: You are right James. He must learn some skills and knowledge to prepare him for the journey.

The Story of the Savior, Jesus of Nazareth

Jesus: I am willing if you can help me. I will repay you when I can.

James: Actually, you can repay us now, because your learning will include working right here.

Levi: James will have all kinds of things for you to do. We are trying to create our own library for the future. We are gathering as much written information as we can. You can help me with that.

James: Lets have Anne, who is a good writer, make a list on papyri of what we want Jesus to do.

Anne returns to the table where the men and the man to be are sitting.

Anne: Mary agreed to take the two little brats... I mean boys.

The men and the man to be laugh.

Levi: Jesus should meet Mary - she is an attractive young lady.

James: And she's smarter than she is attractive. I wish I were eighteen again.

Anne: James, how could you say that? Maybe I will look for an older man like Levi.

Levi: Thanks, James; you're giving me a chance.

The Teacher Must Be Taught

James reaches to Anne and pulls her to him. She goes willingly and they embrace. He strokes her long black beautiful hair.

James: That happens only in my mind. You are for real.

Jesus thinks to himself. This James is a person I would like to be like. How did he get this way? He's so independent yet he doesn't make you jealous of him. He teaches you even when he is not trying to teach you.

James: Anne, we thought you could write down some of our thoughts on how Jesus could become another Melchizedek. Could you go to the supply room and get some ink and pens for writing? Maybe Jesus can go with you to help bring it back.

Off go Jesus and Anne to get the tools to outline a destiny for a young man who thinks big. Anne and Jesus go to the next building. On the way they see Mary playing with Aaron and Isaac. Mary has made some lines in the dirt and they are hopping around and having fun.

Anne: Mary, come here - I want you to meet Jesus.

Mary runs over with the two pranksters following close behind.

Anne: Jesus this is Mary. Mary this is Jesus of Nazareth.

Mary (smiling): Can anything good come out of Nazareth?

The Story of the Savior, Jesus of Nazareth

Anne: Yes, here's an example.

Jesus (looking confused): What's so bad about Nazareth?

Mary: Everybody says that the people of Nazareth are just the same as slaves to the Roman enclave near Nazareth.

Jesus: That's why I'm here. I couldn't stand it any longer. All they do is work for the Romans. Someone has to free them.

Mary: They can only be free if they want to.

Anne: And the Romans make it very hard to want to. You pay big to escape their greedy clutches.

Mary: Most stupid men just fall in line. I'm not interested in men like that. They bore me.

Jesus: My mother's name is Mary.

Mary: Does she know you are here?

Jesus: She doesn't know where I am, but she helped me leave.

Mary: Your father wouldn't have approved?

Jesus: He would not have let me go. I would have died working for the Romans. He's alive but he's dead, or might as well be.

Mary: He's not a man of adventure like you?

The Teacher Must Be Taught

Jesus: An adventure to him is going to Jerusalem for a holy day. He brings animals to sacrifice for his sins.

Mary: His sin is ignorance.

Anne: Now Mary. You don't even know him.

Mary: Yes, I do. I had the same kind of father. And my mother didn't help me get away. I had to run away in the middle of the night. I was sick of being ignorant. You can kill me, but I won't stay here and be ignorant.

Aaron (starts screaming): He kicked dirt at me. He kicked dirt in my face.

Mary: Isaac, you little ... (She grabs Isaac by the arm)

Isaac: He started it Mary, he called me stupid.

Mary: Aaron did you call Isaac stupid?

Aaron: Yes, but it was only because he said something stupid.

Mary: Aaron, what did he say?

Aaron: I don't remember.

Mary: Isaac, what did you say that he thought was stupid? Maybe you offended him?

Isaac: I don't remember.

Anne: I've heard that before. Come Jesus, we must get our supplies and get back to James and Levi.

The Story of the Savior, Jesus of Nazareth

Jesus and Anne head for the supply room while Mary leads Isaac and Aaron off chasing butterflies.

Back now at the Community Room minds begin to buzz with ideas. Execution of ideas is the hard part. How that execution happens can spell big differences in one's life, one's destiny.

James: Here are my ideas for the first two years.

1.) Jesus becomes an expert horseman and learns to train and care for horses.
2.) Jesus becomes an expert builder. He does not just work. He understands arches and pillars and footings and ground and drainage. He doesn't just pound nails, he knows how to build a building.
3.) Jesus studies Hebrew writings, he studies the writings of the "masters" from the far distant east.

Levi (interrupting): Should he learn how to write dot-dash language for the Great Way?

James: I was about to come to that, Levi.

James (again): Jesus should learn how to write dot-dash language.

Jesus: I don't even know what the Great Way is, and I've never heard of dot-dash language.

James: You can converse with anyone with dot-dash language. It's groupings of dots and dashes in sequences that mean something. One grouping might mean where to find the next watering hole. Another combination means horses, and so on. The ancients had to figure these things out to survive. The Chinese written languages are, in many cases, similar to the

The Teacher Must Be Taught

Aramaic written languages of the west that we know. The individual characters are tiny drawings of things common in every day life. Because there were so many different cultures along the Great Way, traders used an even older means of communication which they call dot-dash. It's about as basic as you can get.

Levi: Jesus must learn healing procedures. Maybe the most important thing he should know is how unfair the world is. People are not born equal. Why some people are born into circumstances that allow them to lead nice easy lives, and others are born into circumstances that keep them struggling we do not know. But as far as we can tell, it has always been this way. The ones who have the power and are rich are few. They keep the masses down and usually separate themselves from the common man.

James: Yes, and the common man typically doesn't do much to help himself out of his lot in life. Hard work and die. Hard work, get married, have children - hard work and die.

Jesus: That's why I left. Life has got to be something more.

James: Jesus will learn how unfair the world is when he sees it. Wait until we get him to Rome and he gets to see first hand the Prince of the World.

Jesus: The Prince of the World?

James: Yes, it was in the writings of Lao-Tzu. I think Lao-Tzu got it from Melchizedek but we will never know. Melchizedek the savior left very little in writing. There are stories passed on about the Order of Melchizedek but very little from his own hand. He came before Abram. You read about him only once in the Law. The Law was eventually taken over by the Levites. And then comes the written history of war. If only Melchizedek could return. Melchizedek thought completely differently than the Prince.

Jesus head was swimming, the Great Way? The Far East? Dot-dash language? Melchizedek? Rome? What had he gotten himself into? Can I handle all this? There's only one way to find out.

James: We're getting way ahead of ourselves. Let's have Anne write down a broad outline, then we will go back and put in particulars.

Levi: How broad?

James: Broad, like first year such and such, second year such and such, and so forth.

Anne: Why don't we make a list of what we think he should learn, then where he should go to learn it and when? What does he do then?

James: He says he wants to save the world.

Levi: That's a pretty broad statement.

James: Maybe the end will become clearer when he gets near the end. Remember that we will then be talking to a different Jesus.

Anne: I hope he doesn't change too much.

James: There is only one way to find out.

The Teacher Must Be Taught

James: I must go water the flowers.

Levi: I think I'll go with you.

James: Jesus, do you want to go?

Jesus: Water the flowers?

James: No, take a piss.

Jesus: Uh ... no, I don't have to go.

James: Anne?

Anne: No thanks, I'll go water my flowers somewhere else when I'm ready.

The two older boys leave. They are serious, but have fun while they are being serious. Is that possible?

Anne: Jesus, you are what age?

Jesus: Fifteen.

Anne: Do you have a girlfriend?

Jesus: Well...

Anne: Well, what?

Jesus: I don't know how to say this Anne, but my biggest problem is well ... you know, I look at young ladies and they look so good to me. Not just as friends, I mean.

Anne: What's the problem?

The Story of the Savior, Jesus of Nazareth

Jesus: I'm not supposed to feel that way.

Anne: You aren't? Who said that?

Jesus: My father.

Anne: You mean the one who works all day long with his head down sweating under the noonday sun for the sake of the Romans?

Jesus: Yes, he says we should be thankful we're not slaves or Roman soldiers sacrificed on the field of battle. At least we get to work. He says we're free.

Anne: Free to do what?

Jesus: I don't know. Just free.

Anne: Don't get me wrong Jesus, your father was a wonderful man to take in your mother like he did while she was bearing someone else's child. But he's not free. Freedom is in the mind.

Jesus: He says you should only have sex to have children, but I see the young men and women of my age. They don't listen.

Anne: How can they, when the urge is greater than the guilt that is laid upon them?

Jesus: It's a problem.

Anne: The problem isn't sex or your narrow-minded, hard working father. Sex is for life. It is a thing of beauty. It is to be honored. The real problem is getting pregnant.

The Teacher Must Be Taught

Jesus: What do you mean, Anne?

Anne: When little fifteen or sixteen year old girls get pregnant they have babies like little boys and little girls. The problem comes in taking care of those babies. Especially boy babies.

Jesus: Why boy babies?

Anne: Read the Law if you haven't already. It is revealed to you there.

Jesus: What is revealed?

Anne: Moses the Levite, a killer, a violent person from the past. The past reveals the present.

Jesus: I have had the Law read to me over and over, but I didn't know this.

Anne: Male babies who grow up without fathers often become violent leaders of society.

Jesus: I didn't know this.

Anne: How could you? You see a violent man today and you don't know where he came from. You don't really know what's going on inside his head.

Jesus: Why is this?

Anne: It has always been this way.

Jesus: Does it always have to be this way?

The Story of the Savior, Jesus of Nazareth

Anne: That is a question for you to answer.

Levi and James return. They stand near the end of the table where Jesus and Anne sit.

James: Two years here at Qumran, six years on the Great Way, back here for a little while, then six years in Rome. That should do it.

Levi: Does pissing help you think?

James: It did that time.

They all laugh as James and Levi sit down again.

James: Now start writing Anne; this is for Jesus at Qumran.

1.) Training horses with the best—Jonas;
2.) "Building" training with Benjamin;
3.) Spiritual practices training with me;
4.) Healing training with Anne;
5.) Knowledge training with Levi, which includes dot-dash writing.

Then two years or so from now he should be ready for a trading caravan on the "Silk Road." He will go to Damascus. He will have such valuable knowledge that he will be able to work for the caravan master. I will write letters of introduction to the Buddhist lamas, and to the followers of Lao-Tzu and the Way that I met over ten years ago on the journey I took with Levi.

Levi: Some of our friends will surely still be there unless some warlord has sacked their Temples.

The Teacher Must Be Taught

James: The warlords seem to stay away from the temples. Not always, but most times. They usually try to convince people to respect their religion unless it threatens the warlord. I think that they think they can get more out of the people that way. Jesus has already started his training with me. Anne what do you think?

Anne: I think he needs to go to Rome and see for himself where most of the troubles come from. The people's problems come from two main sources. The natural world and the world of humans. The world of humans is more devastating to the people than the natural world.

Levi: Well said, Anne.

Jesus: What would I do in Rome?

James: Learn about the Roman Emperor and his "system."

Jesus: Who is he?

James: It doesn't matter. They are all the same. Oh, one might be a little better or a little worse than another, but you have no way of knowing. Most of them would send their mothers into slavery if it were worth anything to them.

Levi: We will make sure you get a job with a good masonry expert in Rome. The Emperors are always building something. They don't know how to do much of anything themselves. They have it done for them. You should be able to get an inside look at the bastards. They live by their army. Whoever controls the best army is the Emperor.

Jesus: Do they run the government?

The Story of the Savior, Jesus of Nazareth

James: Indirectly. They have the power to do what they want. They have others do it for them.

Jesus: How do we get out of this mess?

James: That's why we're sending you to become the Melchizedek of today. You will read Isaiah like you've never read it before. You will meditate with the masters. You will become an artisan. Then you will be able to suggest ideas to the people who are in bondage. Is this not what you've wanted?

Jesus: I am compelled from within. I have no choice in the matter. I have to know.

Levi: You do have a choice, Jesus. You are on dangerous ground. You will be exposed to killers. They will laugh at you as they strangle you.

Jesus: Somebody has got to do it!

James: Lots of people have tried. Most never get anywhere. Hopefully you will be so well trained that you might be different.

Words and emotions. The desire to change the world played out in the mind. A good feeling comes when the disadvantaged envision justice in the world. The teachers of Qumran all say that the first thing you need to know is that the world is not fair. If you expect it to be fair you are fodder. Alas, most justice is played out in the mind not reality. The disadvantaged accept their lot in life. Everyone cannot be the Emperor. There is only one of him. Winner takes all in life's game. Well, not all. The winner needs the losers, to be in fact, the winner.
At Qumran James read the Septuagint to Jesus in Greek. Then, he read the Hebrew Law, Prophets, and Writings. He

The Teacher Must Be Taught

told Jesus that he must somehow imagine himself going back in time. The writers of these great works, said James, were real people. They had something to say. What were they trying to say? Then think about the world of today. Do you see the problems today that you read about from the past? The past creates the future. The future is not independent of the past. James told Jesus that the present moment is like a platform sitting upon a giant pile of something. You stand on the platform. You dance. You look out over the world. How solid are the underpinnings of the platform upon which you stand?

James told Jesus how the Jews had used the Law, the Prophets, and the Writings to bind the people together. The Jews had a common bond; otherwise they were just like everybody else. James also told Jesus that many Jews of today disagreed upon what the Law, the Prophets, and the Writings had to say to the people of today. The Pharisees didn't agree with the Sadducees; the Essenes didn't agree with either one of them. James told Jesus that there was just as much bad in the Septuagint, maybe more, than there was good. The Levites had allowed some of Melchizedek's thought, but it was censored. This was a cover for the Levites, he told Jesus. They all were still Jews. They were enemies from within, said James, but they now had a greater enemy - the Romans. The Romans sought to subjugate the Jews. Just as the twelve tribes of Israel had fought with one another for dominance, now comes something even worse - the Emperor. The ultimate killing machine is at his disposal. James told Jesus that he would find hatred in the Law, Prophets, and Writings, and he would find love. It was as if human kind was searching, groping in the darkness. As if seeking the light. Who was the true God? The Emperor claimed he was from God, or was God. The characters from the Law, the Prophets, and the Writings all claimed to be writing or speaking from "God's lips." The same God one day would command you to kill women, children, and the unborn, and the next day tell you not to kill. How could this be?

The Story of the Savior, Jesus of Nazareth

James taught Jesus how to meditate every day. He taught him how to pray every day. Prayer was personal. Go to your private place. Jesus built his own altar of stones. He would go there to either meditate or pray. James taught Jesus about the "levels" of prayer, starting at the bottom with selfish prayer and going up the scale to the "communion" with El, Jaweh, Tao, the Divine Buddha, or God. He taught Jesus that we can and must know part of God. We come away with that knowledge in the communion of prayer. To think that we know all of God might be hubris. The Prince of the World has succumbed to hubris. When Melchizedek said, "I and the Father are one," he meant that he thought like the Father when he was at his highest level of humanhood. He could speak the Father's wishes for the good of mankind. Never, never did Melchizedek claim to be God.

Jesus learned about fasting. He would only drink water or fruit juices for 2 or 3 days. Jesus found his mind to be sharper sometimes when he fasted. Spontaneous thoughts would "pop" into his mind. Thoughts he had never had before. Jesus felt it was also spurred by his concentrated efforts on reading the thoughts of the most intelligent minds from Levi's library.

Jesus' mind was baffled by the incongruities of life. Nothing made sense to him except power. Who had power and how long could they keep it. The world teeter-tottered like the teeter-totter that Isaac and Aaron played on. Might makes right. Not quite, but most of the time. James had asked Jesus not only to read the works of the great writers but to try to go inside their minds. When he did this he concluded that not all these works attributed to a great writer came from the same mind. Isaiah and the Psalms might have been his favorites. He knew deep within him that all the verses in them were not all from the same mind. What does James think of this? Politics, James would say. When the books of the Law, the Prophets, and the Writings were canonized by the elders of the Jewish

The Teacher Must Be Taught

hierarchy, they needed to agree on what to canonize. James told Jesus that the Greek Septuagint was an effort to do this; to take all the Hebrew writings and consolidate them. Therefore, an accepted version of history's writings would be less confusing. Ah, this made sense. Yes, in order to have a Jewish conformity of thought, you must have something to conform to. In order to understand the Septuagint one had to understand politics.

Chapter Four
One Year Later

James: Jesus, its the middle of the night! What are you doing up? It will soon be time to greet the rising sun.

Jesus was sitting at the table with rolls of papyrus stretched out with weights sitting on them, to keep them from scrolling back up.

Jesus: I catch snoozes during midday when the sun's the hottest and I wouldn't be doing or learning much anyway. In the middle of the night the daily chores are not a weight on me or my mind. I am free to use my entire mind. Just so I can stay awake. It takes time and practice and some of Anne's strongest tea or coffee.

James: You are learning aren't you? There are plants and herbs that can stimulate you. There are others that can kill you. It's all in knowing the difference.

James (again): I see that you have side by side here portions of the works of the Psalmists and the works of the Isaiahs.

Jesus: I have read them over and over. I never tire of them. Each time I read them they seem to speak to me in a little different way.

James: Can you live with confusion?

Jesus: I must.

One Year Later

James: You do not eliminate confusion with words but only with deeds. That is what Isaiah says. That is what the psalmists say. They cry out for another Melchizedek, a Savior of the World.

Jesus: They seem to define what God is.

James: They do that too.

James (again): You would do well, Jesus, to make the Psalms and Isaiah a part of you. To think like them.

Jesus: I do, but I must convert these noble thoughts to action.

James: I hope you can keep that desire through your period of apprenticeship. You must have all the tools you need to combat the Prince of Darkness who controls the world.

Jesus: I am impatient.

James: Good!

James (again): I also notice that you and Mary have become friends. Are you also lovers?

Jesus: She does not want to be pregnant until after I am done with my training, so we are careful as we can be.

James: That's a long time to wait. Can you handle the urge?

Jesus: I don't know if I can. She wants to go on my journey east. She says she can't take the chance of losing me. The urge to procreate brings forth new life, new souls for the

The Story of the Savior, Jesus of Nazareth

journey to greater life. I must teach what a greater life is. In the meantime we will be careful. She and I have talked about this many times.

James: She is a beautiful woman.

Jesus: She is more beautiful on the inside. I could not bear to be without her. She must come with me. We will make it somehow.

James: You won't if she gets pregnant.

Jesus: We can do it. I know we can.

James: When you go to Rome it might not be so bad. It is not so far away. When traveling over the Great Sea from Caesarea Maritime, you may be only one-week's time away from home. The Far East is easily a one-year journey.

Jesus: Why must I go so far? Why must I have such a long apprenticeship?

James: To learn the difference between free will and coercion, and then to decide what God has to say about them, if anything. Then, you must make a great decision - which pathway you will take. You must learn from people as well as writings. You must learn from experience.

Jesus: I don't understand.

James: You shouldn't yet. But you will - it must come to you. If you go at it with all your heart and soul it will come to you. If you knock on its door, it will open the door.

Jesus: What is "it?"

One Year Later

James: The Way, the Great Way. The tree of Life. The moving front. The Tao.

Jesus: You talk in mysteries.

James: You will too.

Chapter Five
Caravan Along the Silk Road

Another year passed. James was right. Jesus did need to learn how to contribute to society with work before he could do anything. But contributing and being a slave, or a slave to work, were two entirely different things. Mary had learned to be quite the healer. She wasn't perfect. She didn't know everything, but she was fascinated by her ability to help others aches and pains with certain combinations of herbs and crushed plants that Anne had taught her. She was excited to learn more of this in the Far East. She also learned how to cook and sew and make clothing for her and Jesus. She knew how to take care of children. And Anne taught her about sex; about this almost ever-present urge the male has if he's older than twelve and younger than seventy. Not very many men lived to be seventy. Only three out of ten made it to twelve. But those that made it wanted as much sex as they could get. If she knew that, then she could live accordingly.

All she wanted in a man she saw in Jesus. She was content to wait until it was right. James called it righteousness. What was right for her and what was right for another woman could be two different things. She loved Jesus so much that she did not want to stand in the way of his destiny. She knew he felt the same about her. She knew because he told her that. She hoped he would not change. Was he right in his thinking? There's only one way to find out. They rode their Arabian horses with a trading caravan from Jerusalem to Damascus. They both were experts in horsemanship. The more you knew about horses, the greater was your mobility.

The caravan master of the caravan to Damascus, Ebeneezer, knew of a Far East caravan master who from his

Caravan Along the Silk Road

youth went back and forth along the "Silk Road." His name was Ak-Bar. Ebeneezer, at the request of James, had lined up jobs for Mary and Jesus with the caravan. They would work for their passage to the Far East. Some caravans had as many as one thousand people. Some people were settlers who dared to brave the uncertainties of the one-year journey in hopes of finding a new home, away from taxes and the Romans. Some people were there for the money. They were traders. There had always been traders and always would be. They brought back treasures from China unknown to the people living on the perimeter of the Great Sea. Some were trying to escape the clutches of the Emperor. Perhaps a Roman government official who dared oppose the Emperor. He knew that he and his family could be found mysteriously dead. It was deadly business being involved in politics with the powerful. Some idealistic young men didn't realize that. Roman soldiers were always checking these caravans for such as they. Their disguises must be good. Only travel as a family when you are out of range of Romans. Some dastardly men made their livings by uncovering runaway Roman "free-citizens."

One family was beheaded in a ritual right in front of the whole caravan, which was forced to a stop by a Roman soldier unit. Ak-Bar was furious but there was nothing he could do. Until he passed the Caucasus Mountains, he was at the will of the Romans. The father, a politician, was accused of plotting against the Emperor. The mother and father, the twelve, ten, and eight-year-old boys, and the six-year-old girl, were beheaded all at the same time. Mary couldn't take it - she would not watch. The caravan hadn't made it one hundred miles from Damascus. It left an indelible mark on the mind and memory of Jesus of Nazareth. Mary vomited until there was nothing left in her to vomit. She knew now she had entered the real world. Jesus wondered whether his stepfather was right. But he had to honor a father he never knew. Besides this was not right. Isaiah was crying out for someone to stand up to this

The Story of the Savior, Jesus of Nazareth

kind of world and stare it down. But how could you prevent this kind of injustice, this cruelty?

Ak-Bar, the caravan master, approached Jesus; the normally jovial man was not in a good mood.

Ak-Bar: Jesus, come with me. I will get two or three other young men to help me bury the bodies of those poor people. The centurions took the heads with them to prove that they had gotten the right ones. Just left the bodies lying there. Those bastards. They don't even have the decency to bury them.

Jesus: How can they do this kind of thing?

Ak-Bar: They are paid assassins. They are under orders. They are soldiers. They think they do this for the "State." The Emperor thinks he is God. That makes everything all right. He does not have to look at them. It's called killing from a distance. The rotten bastard Emperor is probably drinking his brains out right now. He will get his someday. I would like to be there to watch his groans. Meanwhile he has sex with any Roman woman he wants. He doesn't even know how many children he has.

Jesus: I will get Thomas and Peter to help us.

Ak-Bar was a delightful Turkish man with a big curled mustache. Jesus loved him even though he was a little rough around the edges. He knew Ak-Bar would stand by you when things were really tough. There weren't very many of these kinds of men.

The caravan master and the three young men did their horrible duty. After the bodies were buried, Jesus asked if he could say a prayer for these people he never knew and who

Caravan Along the Silk Road

didn't deserve this fate. He knew that they did not deserve this fate. They all bowed their heads.

Jesus: Great Power of the Universe, I sit in the morning and let the rays from your Sun give me energy. The Sun gives its energy to everyone without questioning whether they are bad or good. Your house contains many Suns. Your ways are not our ways. Help us to understand this paradox that lies before us, covered with dirt. As these souls have not been honored here on earth, we ask that you honor them in heaven, Amen.

Ak-Bar, Thomas and Peter's heads pop up.

Thomas: There is no heaven.

Ak-Bar: Now let's get back to our jobs. We have a huge caravan to get moving. Get on your horses, boys. I will go to the head wagons to get them moving. You boys ride to the rear to let them know we will be moving until the Sun is two Suns from the western horizon.

The caravan's head started moving. It took the tail longer to get moving. Soon it was like a giant caterpillar, wending and winding its way eastward to a far off Shangri-La that meant a new home for some, and silk and jade, tea and artifacts like none other seen in the western world for others. The treasures they brought back were worth the price of the journey. Jesus and his beloved Mary were more interested in the treasures of the mind and spirit; non-corruptible treasures that could not be taken from them. Once learned and imbedded in the labyrinth of the mind, they were yours for interactions with others and to serve you. To make you more competent. A blessing to your neighbor. They were searching for treasures from Heaven.

The Story of the Savior, Jesus of Nazareth

The initial incident of the executions of the Roman family was the worst that happened on the journey. Others died, as is expected on these long journeys. Some from sickness. A couple died from mishaps while fixing wagons. None died from thieves. The Roman Army had put the fear of God in to those who impeded the trading routes. The Romans wanted their supply of goods from the east flowing like a river. Jesus and Ak-Bar grew to be close friends. Jesus delighted in Ak-Bar's big smile, his sense of humor and more than anything his artisanry. He combined artisanry with compassion. True artisanry thought Jesus includes the idea of compassion. Ak-Bar's front wagon was loaded with "star-charts."

Ak-Bar: I learned to navigate on the Great Sea, Jesus. The ancients noticed the procession of the stars. The stupid of the world notice nothing. The world is round just like the moon, just like the stars. We live in a vast Seaway beyond our comprehension. We are but little children in God's home. Jesus you would do well to notice the heavens. Look at them. Listen to them. If you are intense enough you can hear them. They twinkle at you. They are you and you are them.

Jesus could listen to this Turkish man for hours on end. He fascinated Jesus. It was as if he was from another world, only visiting this one. Learning something, yet conveying more than he was learning.

Jesus: I wish to be like you, Ak-Bar.

The horses towing the wagon swatted flies with their tales. They had been pastured overnight and were well watered. The "Silk Road" was home to lots of animal manure. If the wind was over its pathway, you were reminded of the baser parts of life as you contemplated the more sublime. Sometimes, if it was too hot, they would rest during the day and travel at

Caravan Along the Silk Road

night. When there was a full moon it was easy. They discovered that one star's light was so bright that it would allow shadows to be cast on the ground. They knew that it wasn't a star because it moved in the sky differently than the stars. What could it be?

Ak-Bar: Learn to love yourself, Jesus. Be sure that you have good reasons for all the work you have done to improve your mind. If you stay on the Great Way, you will have much to share with humanity. Build your life, Jesus. Make it something worthwhile. You will find that there are all kinds of ways to skin a cat.

Jesus: Skin a cat?

Ak-Bar: It's an expression. Don't take it literally. It means that there are all kinds of ways to end up with a result. Some good, some bad, most in-between.

Jesus: Ak-Bar, do you ever have a non-sensical conversation?

Ak-Bar: Only by accident.

Jesus laughs, Ak-Bar laughs. Now things are good. The morning is cool. The afternoon will be hot. There will be more of a premium on getting through the afternoon, both for the humans and the animals.

The humans could not make the journey without the animals. They were depended on. Ak-Bar maybe didn't skin cats, but he skinned deer, he skinned sheep, he skinned bears, he skinned all kinds of animals. Those on the caravan ate them. They needed them for transportation. They needed them for clothing and shoes. Jesus' horse was a friend; Mary's horse was a friend.

The Story of the Savior, Jesus of Nazareth

Jesus: You said you learned to navigate on the Great Sea.

Ak-Bar: At night - I learned to navigate when it was clear. Cloudy weather was no good. In storms, we could not see the stars.

Jesus: How do the stars help you?

Ak-Bar: The North Star never moves Jesus. It is my friend of friends. The Greek constellations move, but not my friend the North Star. I also have this strange device mounted on my cart. It's a piece of metal that is allowed to rotate freely. It always points north. I learned this from the Chinese.

Ak-Bar (again): It is like the Way. The North Star and my star charts are my external guidance system. My internal guidance system is the Way.

Jesus: James the Righteous had me read the Writings of the teachers of the Way while I lived at Qumran.

Ak-Bar: The ancient one, Melchizedek, taught the Great Way to the Chinese. Ancient legends now lost say that Melchizedek moved from Gaul over the Great Sea, and then through Turkey to the Silk Road. He then made his home in the great Oases around the great Gobi desert. He went there with his people, to get away from the warlords taking over society.

Jesus: Why did he need to move, Ak-Bar?

Ak-Bar: He was an artisan and quester of knowledge - humanity's accumulated wisdom. He was smart. I base my feelings toward life on his. He was an architect of buildings, a

Caravan Along the Silk Road

mason. He also was a builder of life. The body, the mind, and the spirit were under construction to Melchizedek. Life's purpose was to learn and serve your fellow human being.

Jesus: This is a fascinating way to look at life.

Ak-Bar: It's a fascinating way to live life. It somehow makes you free.

Jesus: The warlords? Could Melchizedek not handle them?

Ak-Bar: In order to bring about the best in society, the individual had to bring about the best in himself. Melchizedek's idea of what was best and what the warlords thought best were two different things.

Ak-Bar (again): The warlords learned that through violence and coercion they could short cut the hard labor of the mind. This is the hardest labor of all Jesus. Learning. You must ingest as much knowledge as you can from the past. You must test that knowledge in reality. Some of the past's knowledge is good, some out-right wrong and most ... well, most is mixed. You must be a sifter of history. You must learn from others. They are the same as us. Their minds can be mined.

Jesus: You are a gold mine, Ak-Bar.

Ak-Bar: I give my gold to you so that you may give it to others, Jesus. That is the way of Melchizedek.

Jesus: I still wonder about Melchizedek and the warlords.

The Story of the Savior, Jesus of Nazareth

Ak-Bar: The warlords forced Melchizedek to work for them. He and his architects built their cities of the west. The warlords got as much out of them as they could.

Jesus: Why didn't Melchizedek take up the sword against them and put them in their place?
Ak-Bar: Some that Melchizedek taught did this. They tried to bluff one another. In the end it escalated to war. One tried to knock the chip off the other's shoulder.

The Wagons rolled along. The herds of horses didn't stray very far. Ak-Bar could find food and water for them. They seemed to know that Ak-Bar could find water better than they could. He told Jesus that he was not the only caravan master, not the only game in town. But he also told him that the masters shared knowledge. It was an unwritten rule. Ak-Bar had hundreds of maps. The Silk Road had more than one route. If one caravan met with some natural disaster, such as a brutal sandstorm, they knew that the next caravan might be only two months behind them. They would then share and band together to complete the trip. The artisans while on these fascinating journeys were not bothered by the warlords. When they settled down to create their own little Shangri-La, they then were subject to confiscation by the men of war.

They passed through what Ak-Bar called the Caucasian Mountains. He would tell Jesus that now the people would start to look a little different. Ak-Bar conversed with all of them through the dot-dash language written in the earth. Some hugged Ak-Bar before they even spoke. Some came along for the journey of the soul. Some even learned Greek and Turkish. Jesus' language skills were improving, but if it weren't for the dot-dash language, he would have been lost.

After ten months on the road, Mary beckoned Jesus from the back of their wagon. The mountains that Ak-Bar spoke of were coming in to view. Jesus mind was still foggy

Caravan Along the Silk Road

from sleep. He rubbed his eyes as Mary pointed to the east. "Oh my, the most beautiful mountains I have ever seen!" The majestic Himalayas were covered with the cleanest, whitest snow he had ever seen. Jesus was struck with awe. He hugged Mary, he kissed Mary. Here they were together, experiencing purple, snow-capped mountains - as majestic as they could be. How fortunate they were. "Mary, I thank God for you, the mountains, and the journey." He felt shivers and joy deep within him. He wished everyone could feel this way. And why couldn't they, he thought.

He now remembered back to his laboring step-father, the spoiled Roman kid with no sense of appreciation, and the captive people of Jerusalem. Captives of a system that they didn't question. What was life? He asked this over and over to himself. Just what is life? Mary gave his hand a squeeze. The Himalayas that lay ahead beckoned his curious spirit. He would go over those mountains to see for himself. And he knew also that he would return someday to Jerusalem, to beckon the spirits of the poor and the enslaved. They too were God's children. He would be their teacher - just as James and Ak-Bar were artisan teachers, so he would be too.

Ak-Bar (He rides up to Jesus and Mary on his black Arabian stallion and jumps into the wagon with them. The black stallion trots alongside without being tethered. He will not leave Ak-Bar.): Jesus, will you join my scouts and me in two days time? We will ride ahead of the caravan to find the pass through and over the mountains. We may have to leave some of our bigger wagons on the west side. We are far to the North of the highest summits. When you visit the Buddhists of the mountains, you will do it from the other side. You will go to them from Xinjan.

Jesus: Mary, do you mind?

The Story of the Savior, Jesus of Nazareth

Mary: Ak-Bar, am I safe?

Ak-Bar: Anyone who harms you knows that he will see my wrath. I don't often get mad, but when I do, you do not want to be there. I wouldn't ask Jesus to do this unless I felt that you would be safe. My sister Meshka will stay with you. She has kicked many a drunk in a way to quickly calm his lust. One drunk, I told his wife about the next day. The rest of the trip was miserable for him.

Chapter Six
Among the Buddhists

The caravan left the big wagons on the western slope. The mules were the real stars of the mountain passes. Sometimes, if the rivers were not dangerous, they would make huge rafts out of logs and float everything through. Other caravans respected the rights of untended wagons. The wagons were dated in dot-dash language. The supplies had all been strapped on the backs of horses, donkeys and camels. The lead men road on mules. Mules were not only the invention of Universe, but also of pilgrims, who had to go over mountain passes. Ak-Bar said that two-hump camels could be found on the eastern side of the great mountains. He wanted to bring several of these back on the trip west. They were ornery animals, but good beasts of burden.

Ak-Bar's artisanry included the taming and training of Chinese camels and horses. He would trade sleek Arabian horses for Chinese horses and two-hump camels. Ak-bar was a trader. He said the Chinese were traders too. Trade must be honorable, said Ak-Bar. One could not come back and have friends if the trading was without honor. He was well aware that there were dishonest western traders. He was well aware that there were dishonest eastern traders. The best business system involved treating one another with respect. Make good on a horse that proves bad. You will come out much better in the long run.

There now were many Caucasians living in the oases around the Takla maken Shomo both to the north and the south. Both the Chinese and Caucasians complained of the dynasty that was located in the place in the Far East near the great ocean. The ancient Melchizedek and the Caucasians before him

The Story of the Savior, Jesus of Nazareth

had filtered into the Takla maken Shomo from the west to escape the warlords who wanted nothing but power. Ancient legends told of how the Chinese and the Caucasians lived in harmony around the desert. They were protected from the Brahmins to the south by the Himalayas. The Caucasian warlords had plenty to do around the Great Sea and Gaul. The Emperors of China ruled the more populated areas of eastern China, along the coastline of the great impenetrable ocean. It was Shangri-La for the ancient ones. When things changed for the worse in 700 B.C., Lao-Tzu started writing about the ancient sages. When things get bad, writers of wisdom write. They attempt to influence the minds of the lost. Jesus came to know the cycles of war and peace. Peace would only last just so long.

Ak-Bar introduced them to his old friend Wa-Lu at Aksay in China. Jesus was the architect and builder of buildings through his training at Qumran. The buildings looked different in China. The principles of building them the same. Mary was a healer, a caregiver for children, and a maker of wonderful recipes for food. Work! Jesus and Mary would work for their livelihoods. Both of them were experts with horses. Wa-Lu would be their sponsor. It got him two of Ak-Bar's Arabian horses, payment for Jesus and Mary for their help on the long journey.

Five years later Jesus would learn Ak-Bar had died. Ak-Bar's sons Antala and Mevlana and his sister Meshka had learned the business and would transport Mary and Jesus back along that same "Silk Road" to Damascus. But first, they would fill the treasure chests of their minds with gold of heavenly quality.

Ak-Bar: Jesus knows the masonry business well Wa-Lu. He is also good with horses and camels. He will not disappoint you. Mary makes the best-roasted meats, fruits, and vegetables over special wood that she finds. She has spices that make my mouth water when I smell them. She is a healer, Wa-Lu. She

Among the Buddhists

can teach you of western healing, and you can acquaint her with the eastern methods. She is very good with children and loves to teach them.

Wa-Lu: Ah, my friend Ak-Bar, someday I may go west with you.

Ak-Bar: Stay here Wa-Lu, the Roman over-lords rule the west like your dynasties rule the east. They are of the same ilk. They become corrupted by power. Someday they may clash somewhere between the two great oceans. They will try to kill each other until only one man stands. Maybe Yomanne` will strike that one with lightening and fry him to a crisp, so that this does not start all over again. The world will be finally saved.

They all laugh as Ak-Bar erupts in laughter.

Wa-Lu: Ak-Bar teaches as Chung-Tzu teaches.

Ak-Bar: I also teach as Buddha or Lao-Tzu.

Wa-Lu: Perhaps Jesus and Mary can save the world, so that people can exist and be happy and lead lives of meaning.

Ak-Bar: If they stay here your dynasties won't let them. If they go back, which they are pledged to do in five years time, the Romans won't let them.

Wa-Lu: Ah! Man's nemesis: himself!

Ak-Bar: Jesus and Mary must learn the spiritual practices of the masters.

The Story of the Savior, Jesus of Nazareth

Wa-Lu: They will be in good hands Ak-Bar; they will know how to excise diseased organs from the body. They will know the diseases of the mind that corrupt the self. They will learn the Tao - the narrow gate to life.

Ak-Bar: They are willing Wa-Lu. They knock on the door.

Wa-Lu: If the son asks the father for a fish will he give him a serpent?

Ak-Bar: And if he asks for bread will he give him a stone?

Wa-Lu: I think not. They are of the Father.

And so it went in the land of metaphors. Jesus and Mary proved to be big contributors to the villages on the perimeter of the desert. Jesus made masonry buildings. He made masonry tombs for the dead in the desert, as the ancient Melchizedek did long ago. Melchizedek the Savior and King of Peace, it is told, returned from the Takla maken Shomo to the west. He founded a city by the name of Salem. He was interested in training peacemakers to save the world. Peacemakers, he said, must be made. It looked like war was becoming the "natural" state of affairs as the bullies of the world usurped the artisans. Someone must stand up to them and gain the support of the people. He said that peacemakers shall be called Sons of God. Did God create all the beautiful variety of people to be subjugated by the few? It could not be this way. At least not if God loved the world.

A year passed, and the people of the little villages on the south of the Takla maken Shomo found that they loved Jesus and Mary. They sponsored a trip of eight months for Mary, Jesus, and Wa-Lu to go hundreds of miles up into the moun-

Among the Buddhists

tains of Xizang, the same mountains that Mary and Jesus had seen from a distance. Wa-Lu said that there may be no better place to learn spiritual practices than at the Buddhist monasteries near Gyangze. Wa-Lu said that the place feeds the spirit, as the spirit feeds the place. He was right. And so they leave on their journey. Three months of the trip pass.

Wa-Lu: Jesus this is the monastery ahead where we will meet the monks of the Buddha.

Jesus had been taught by Wa-Lu that the Buddha was a real person who was born into a wealthy upper-caste family in India. As he was being taught Brahminism, which was anchored in the ancient Way, he noticed that the reality of today's society did not conform to its underlying ideals. Reality overwhelmed idealism. Idealism was a confabulation of the organic self. A wish, a hope, perhaps. Somehow, when lived out, it tended towards mine-verses-yours. And that meant - it's mine, not yours.

The little birds in the nest squawk like crazy when the mother comes back with a worm. The biggest squawkers get the worm. The solitary little frail one (how did he get born into frailty?) didn't get food, except when the others were full. Same mother, same father, the eggs looked the same but they were not the same. One source, different results. Do you blame the aggressive chick? What does he know? Do you blame the frail chick? What does he know? The mother doesn't seem to know either. How does this happen? The little one is left in the nest. Alone. To die of starvation. Or be eaten by a crow, or a snake. Do birds reflect on this conundrum? He doubted it. Do humans reflect on this conundrum? Gautama Sidharta did. His father and mother said that he was born to be superior. The dirty poor ones. The beggars were born to be that way. Perhaps.

The Story of the Savior, Jesus of Nazareth

It bothered him so much, that he left the upper crust and their cozy lives. If that's life, he decided, I don't want it. Settling into a system of thoughtlessness. He was to find mindfulness - the way of the Mind. These people of today had lost the Way. Was he only reading of the ideals of the past, and were they, in reality, that way too? Perhaps. But he had to find out for himself. No one else's words or teachings could do it. He must know. If it killed him he must know. He vowed to become self-taught and think for himself. He decided that, as part of his training, he would seek out the smartest minds in the world.

Wa-lu, Mary and Jesus would learn and meditate with the monks of the Buddha. In the serene atmosphere of the temples, high in the mountains. The smells, the burning candles, and the "emptiness" of the mind brought the travelers to a higher level. What was the highest level that an earthly human could attain? A question for the spirit, prodded by the soul. Jesus and Mary learned about what the Buddha learned on his journey.

Jesus: The monks are happy people Mary. Jerusalem isn't happy - it's gloomy, it's sad. When we enter the temple and smell the incense, it is as if we are in a different world. The candles and the sounds of the monks as they meditate. When we go out after one day of being with them, I feel like my mind has been cleansed.

Mary: Could you stay here your whole life like them?

Jesus: I could not, but that doesn't mean that they can't. We are all delightfully different they have told me. Different but the same. We must give thanks for our differences and enjoy them.

Among the Buddhists

Wa-Lu: Joy, comes from other people, Jesus, not from things.

Jesus also learned to fast. There was something about not eating for a few days and drinking lots of water that seemed to engage reaches of your mind that you didn't know were there. Ask your mind for something, Wa-Lu, would say. If you were "in tune," answers or thoughts would pop in from nowhere. New thoughts, fresh thoughts. Repeat them to yourself, over and over. Lodge them in your memory. They would stay there for you.

Wa-Lu: Jesus, you must try to remember your dreams at night. Practice this, after awhile you will be able to remember your dreams. Sometimes they pop in and visit you out of nowhere. Melchizedek was a dreamer who acted upon his dreams.

Jesus: Have you read the Septuagint Wa-Lu?

Wa-Lu: No, What is the Septuagint?

Jesus: Just as you have your prophets, the Jews from where I come have theirs. Melchizedek came before Abram. Abram begot Isaac, and Isaac begot Jacob. Jacob begot twelve sons - one of whom, Joseph, was a dreamer. His dreams turned out to be real. Joseph might be my favorite character from the Septuagint.

Jesus, Mary and Wa-Lu sojourned in the mountains of Xizang for a few months meeting the lovely people with big smiles. Maybe that is where the adventuresome Ak-Bar learned his big smile. They studied the thoughts of the Buddha. The earthly Gautama had taken on a divine nature with his "Awakening," just like Melchizedek. They seemed in legend what Ak-

The Story of the Savior, Jesus of Nazareth

Bar seemed in reality. Here, right here, in reality - but answering to the beat of a different drummer. A heavenly drummer. There is something "More," thought Jesus. Another plane, accessible now, through the "narrow gate." On the other side of the gate lay a more abundant sense of life itself.

Wa-Lu: While we are here in the mountains, you must learn the law of Buddha.

Jesus: The Jews have their law, Wa-Lu.

Wa-Lu: Buddha's "Law" was not of his creation. It was the Way, which had been grasped by the ancients. Buddha said, "don't look to me, this is not my Law." Buddha has come down from heaven. The Law is eternal. It is from the Universe.

Jesus: Moses came down from the mountain, Mt. Sinai, to give his people the Law. He was a Levite, a man of war; his laws were to control his people.

Wa-Lu: Ah, Jesus! The idea is coming down from a higher sphere to the world of reality. Your Moses gave it to the people, as Buddha grasped the Eternal and gave it to the unenlightened masses. Laws can be meant to control or laws can be meant to free, by either the receiver or giver.

Wa-Lu: The lawgiver is of the people, but above them and comes back to teach them. He walks with the people.

Jesus: In the real world of the west the Roman overlords do not walk among the people nor do they teach them. They enslave them. They have law and laws but there is no enlightenment in them.

Among the Buddhists

Wa-Lu: The Law of Buddha was meant to free you. Its grasp liberates you, for by its exercise you are not constrained, but liberated. Somehow the mighty become blinded. The law constrains the masses, while the mighty are corrupted by their very power.

Jesus: According to the Buddha, what was the Law?

Wa-Lu: You tread on treacherous ground. The Law is not an end in itself. It is similar to the spiritual practices of meditation, fasting and prayer. You are not saved by them, nor are you saved by the Law. They lead you to the Way, which is "being the process". Everything is in process. You with it and it with you.

Jesus: What is the way of the Law then?

Wa-Lu: You do well when you do not kill, you do not steal, you do not become overpowered with sex, you do not lie, you do not inebriate yourself, you do not slander, you do not abuse others in speech, you do not covet, you do not bear malice, and you do not cling to false views.

Jesus: Shouldn't people already know these? They seem so obvious.

Wa-Lu: Hah! Nothing is obvious.

Jesus: Everybody lies all the time, Wa-Lu. The Jewish Law of not bearing false witness against thy neighbor is not the same as lying.

Wa-Lu: The ancients talked more of righteousness, right thinking, right actions. They are brewed up from within the self. The inner guidance system that one develops inside, in

The Story of the Savior, Jesus of Nazareth

the far recesses of the mind. It is as if you must go in to your quiet place, your room. You then shut your door and pray to the Father in the secret place. Only you and the Universe. Your unspoken thought becomes in this solitude "Show me the Way." No blame or shame is laid on anyone else - it is the you and the It. You two are one. You are the object and the subject. Once you accept responsibility for the you and the It, then you must not stay in the "secret" place. You must arise; go into the world. Bring harmony to a discordant world. You must make the notes into a beautiful melody.

Jesus: It somehow seems so right here amongst the lamas. I am going to Rome someday. It will be different there.

Wa-Lu: I have been to the big cities of the east. They crawl with people. You never see the same one twice. The Dynasty rules with a tight fist, to keep the throngs in order. To them, the Law controls and sustains their position. They remove themselves from the masses and become deities unto themselves.

The learners breathed in the fresh clean air of the mountains; the sky itself seemed more deeply blue.

Jesus: The Bhagavad Gita scriptures that you gave me to read speak of order in society. The ideal of order and the reality of order seen in the cities take on a different character. Here in the mountains it is different. A higher plane.

Wa-Lu: Yes, that is why the Buddha left India and came in to the mountains. You know that Melchizedek, who you say founded Salem in your land, also founded cities of peace in China. The artisans governed society. Everyone was expected to learn at least one trade. The superior took care of the inferior. His ancient words were, "Come unto me all you

Among the Buddhists

laborers, I will give you rest. Learn from me." You see Melchizedek knew just about everything there was to know. He watched over them like a mother hen. They grew in their abilities under his tutelage.

Jesus: There were no warlords?

Wa-Lu: Come Jesus, our conversation wanders. We must meet with the lamas and bid them good-by. We must return to the low country.

With that the travelers headed back to one of the Buddhist temples. Jesus hoped that he could come back someday but he knew within him that it was unlikely. Mary had learned new healing techniques from the monks. Healing and soothing of the mind was as important as the healing and soothing of the body.

The trip down the mountain was easier, but they still had a long way to go. There was a lot of time for talks beside campfires. The supplies of dried food, carried by the extra mule, held up well. Their tents were sturdy. Bathing in cold mountain water was exhilarating, but baths were short. Wa-Lu was an expert archer, and fresh venison cooked over dying embers and spiced with Mary's special concoctions was excellent. They would sit and look at the stars at night. The air was pure and cool. Some nights, if they stayed up late enough, they would lay back on the grass and watch "shooting" stars. Some would leave a trail of smoke. Wa-Lu told of an ancient story where one of these shooting stars had hit the earth. A large hole was found, but no remnant of the star. Trees were scorched for miles around. Some wondered if these brought seeds of life from somewhere else. But what life could sustain the scorching heat?

They remembered the lamas and the people of the high mountains. They seemed so unusually happy. The lamas had

The Story of the Savior, Jesus of Nazareth

laws that they imposed on themselves that were more difficult than the laws brought down from Heaven by the Buddha for the people. It was as if to say, "If we abide by even tougher rules, surely you people can abide by the simpler laws of the Buddha." Buddha was recapturing the Way of the Brahmins that had somehow been lost over time. To Jesus, Buddha was ancient. The Buddha talked about ancients, more ancient than he, who taught the Way. Somehow the Way becomes corrupted by man himself. How does this happen? What can we do about it? Jesus had more questions then he had answers. He really grilled Wa-Lu on the subject of the ancient King of Peace, Melchizedek. James had talked of Melchizedek. But there was only one reference to him in the Law of the Hebrews. Jesus had to know. Mary didn't. Jesus didn't love her any the less for it. They were different. And Jesus was glad for it.

One day while they neared the end of their journey downward they sat beside a mountain stream that, now in the lower elevations, had become a small river. Water to nourish plants and animals near the edge of the Takla maken Shomo.

Wa-Lu: The Chinese Dynasties that have warred for centuries were not a threat to the peaceful society here between the Great Mountains and the Great Desert. Melchizedek had come here to escape the warlords of your world, Jesus. Little did he know that the Chinese warlords would one day take his cities of peace here in China? Caravan masters, and their traders, kept telling him of the terrible carnage occurring in the lands of his birth. Something compelled him to go back. The people all loved him here. Legend has it that they mourned for one month when he left. But he had always stressed that they must learn to take care of one another. He always reminded them that he was merely one of them with an unusual love of life. They too could love life if they ceased worrying about their own selfish welfare all the time. He told them that, as they lost themselves, they would gain a new life. He always talked in

Among the Buddhists

paradox. But here he was an example to them. He left his beautiful wives and children, his many friends, to try to put a stop to war.

Jesus: Was he the founder of the Way?

Wa-Lu: Legend is at a loss here, Jesus. My guess is that Melchizedek had teachers just like we have in today's world. But you by now would know what the Buddha would say.

Jesus: The Way belongs to the people. Buddha is the messenger.

Wa-Lu: The seduction of power must be controlled. It must be spread out among the people. The very power that strains to give life ends up taking it away. God makes his sun shine on the just and the unjust.

Jesus: I was taught that at Qumran. He also sends his rain on the evil and the good.

Wa-Lu: Paradox. Can you live with paradox?

Jesus: There is a Way that threads the needle.

Wa-Lu: You begin to sound like the Buddha or Melchizedek himself. When we get back to the low country I will help you study Lao-Tzu, Chung Tzu and Sun Tzu. That's about all I can do to honor my commitment to my friend Ak-Bar. I just want you to know that had I known you, your spirit, and your thirst I would have helped you without the commitment to Ak-Bar.

The two friends hugged one another beside the River out of Heaven. The air was fresh with smells of budding life.

The Story of the Savior, Jesus of Nazareth

Butterflies floated with the breeze, dragonflies zoomed about in their little quests for mosquitoes. Far in the distance lay the foreboding desert. Jesus noted that the "best life zone" lay somewhere between the peaks of the Himalayas and the Takla maken Shomo. Journeys through the mountains and journeys through the desert ended with stays in the life zone. Home, where was "Home"? Jesus thought. We go on journeys of discovery. We come back home. Life is both.

Mary: (Hair wet and clothing wet): Hey! Let's get to work. I'm getting anxious to get back home. I've got to get back to the children or I will go crazy.

Wa-Lu (Jesus and Wa-Lu are laughing): Yes, and after you've been with them for two days you will wish that you were back here.

Jesus hugs a drenched Mary.

Jesus: Wa-Lu, lets you and I take a dip in the water before we break camp.

Mary watched from a small hill overlooking the crystal clear river of life, as the two splashed and frolicked in the pool just off the main current. They would push each other under. Then one would submerge and swim under water to the other tickling him in the sides. They were having so much fun. Mary did not want to interrupt them. They laughed and played until they were exhausted. Mary had put a long grass stem in her mouth, the seeds swayed at the tip to the tune of the balmy breeze. She was suspended in space and time. How could life be so good, she thought, here in a far distant land? Back in Jerusalem she knew things would still be miserable. Couldn't she and Jesus just stay here, have children, swim in the clear waters and enjoy all these wonderful people? Why did

Among the Buddhists

Jesus have to save the world? He was always talking about the injustice of the world. What about the injustice to her? She decided that life was paradoxical. Perhaps she would understand someday. At this particular moment she did not. Why leave Heaven?

Chapter Seven
The Lessons of the Taoists

Wa-Lu and Jesus were sitting in the library built by Ashkenazy, reminiscing about their trip to the lamas and the feelings of calmness and serenity that came from them and their environment. The feeling was one of a deep oneness with life and each other. Their way was a calm approach to the dealings of the Universe. Other approaches, where the individuated mind seemed to be at odds with the Universe and fighting with its every part, were melted away in the smells, the resonating sounds, and the internal stillness found in the temples of the lamas.

Wa-Lu: Before we study Lao-Tzu, Chung Tzu and Sun Tzu, I need to talk to you about some abstract ideas that I have trouble defining with exactitude.

Jesus: James the Righteous and I had similar conversations at Qumran. I almost know what you are about to say.

Wa-Lu (smiling): Some of us think this way and some of us think like warlords or emperors. Can we live together?

Jesus: We must be reconciled - like the reconciliation of our own minds. Reconciliation like peacemaking is a full time job. Perhaps our destinies are pulled from the magnetism of these ideas.

Wa-Lu: Humans live out abstractions and materialize them into action. Energy wishes to be expressed.

The Lessons of the Taoists

Wa-Lu (again): My first idea is that the spirit of community must be built. It does not seem to perpetuate itself naturally. Our library is an example. We have thousands and thousands of records here. We have cooking recipes. Do you know that the ancient Melchizedek performed operations on humans, live humans, to cure disorders? Not all of them worked. Most didn't. But some people's lives were saved. Drawings showing these procedures are saved here. Remedies for all kinds of illness are saved. We are just scratching the surface of our ability to help one another. Our environment provides us with the most unlikely of tools. Plants that we might ordinarily think of us weeds may have benefit. Some will cure you; some will kill you.

Jesus: The sun itself. The giver of warmth to us can either cure us or kill us.

Wa-Lu: Exactly. It's all in knowing when and how to use our environment. This accumulated knowledge must be stored and given over to mankind, to enhance our lives and the lives of those who will live in the future.

Jesus: I am helping my friend Levi build a library at my home in Qumran.

Wa-Lu: The second point I would like to make is that I have this strong feeling that the Universe is one level of many levels of existence. In our state of humanness we describe some as being higher than others. I, the sage, cannot express the levels concretely. A simplistic example would be that a tree is on a higher level than a rock.

Jesus: And a cow is on a higher level than a tree.

Wa-Lu: And a human is on higher level that a cow.

The Story of the Savior, Jesus of Nazareth

Jesus: And within humans there are higher and higher levels of existence and consciousness.

Wa-Lu: Yes.

Jesus: Is this good or bad?

Wa-Lu: In one sense good, in that it gives the Universe the variety it seems to crave. In another sense, we listen to music and we are attracted to music in harmony. We are repelled by music in discordance.

Jesus: It is obvious to me that we are builders of structures that we all live with and live by. We must build them to be in harmony.

Wa-Lu: Yes, and just as vitally the harmony must be maintained so the one who chimes the bell at the proper time chimes the right bell or has not fallen asleep. We have the power to create and we have the power to maintain.

Wa-Lu (again): Another point is that of God itself, or our perception of the Power.

Jesus: We do not know all of God, but we know some of God.

Wa-Lu: Well put, perhaps God is unveiling creation over time. We partake in its majesty.

Jesus: We awaken ever so slowly as the Universe awakens.

Wa-Lu: And God's greatest gift?

The Lessons of the Taoists

Jesus: The double-edged sword, our free will.

Wa-Lu: Exactly, it all boils down to that. It decides what smells good, what music pleases the ears, what poetry of nature pleases the eye. You could go on and on.

Jesus: It is as if we are the object and the subject.

Wa-Lu: We are. We are the object and the subject. If something hurts us it is bound to hurt others like us. If something seems good to us chances are it feels good to someone else.

Jesus: This is an extraordinary ability. I can talk to myself.

Wa-Lu: Yes, and you can say "Is what I am doing the right thing to do?"

Jesus: I think some people never ask the question. They are afraid of what they might think about themselves.

Wa-Lu: This brings me to my next point. I am a student of history, Jesus. I can tell you that human history has been one of warfare. We live right now in a bubble here at the base of the Takla maken Shomo. I am no fool, one day this Library may well be destroyed by a warlord on his way to becoming an Emperor. Lao-Tzu calls him "The Prince of this World." Many hundreds of years ago, some men found that they could control the free will of others. Melchizedek, the artisan, the peacemaker, said that anything coming to you by other than someone's free will is not coming from God. One part of the whole seeks to dominate other parts in the awakening process. The bullies who do not have much talent themselves have found that through fear and violence they could control the artisans, artists, and thinkers who were the biggest contributors to

The Story of the Savior, Jesus of Nazareth

society. After Melchizedek, the artisans formed guilds to protect them from the bully. The Dynasties here in China fight amongst themselves to determine who will be the top dog. They then rule by force of arms.

Jesus: The same thing has happened in the west. At Qumran I studied the past and found that my own people succumbed to the way of war after the patriarch Jacob. Their religion was usurped by a man of war, Moses. Thereafter, the peacemakers were subjugated by the Levites. The rules of war that I read at Qumran came from the priests of the religion itself. Thus war was condoned by the very ones who should have been preaching against it.

Wa-Lu: The Prince of the World rules by stealth and cunning. He sends the innocents to death in battle while he revels in his patriotism. A hypocrite is the Prince.

Jesus: I have thought over and over about this problem of why society is so unbalanced. Why does war persist? Why does violence persist? Finally one night under the stars a shooting star went by overhead - it momentarily lit up the sky as if it were the middle of the day. Then back to darkness and I still could see the smoke from its trail. Humans are naturally this way, I said to myself. There can be no other answer. How much evidence do you need? Compassion has been overruled by cold, hard economics. You get results faster by the exercise of violence. It is a short cut to results that could be won over the long term by the Way. In fact, the results are different. The bully chooses to use coercion. He represents the few. The many are like a herd of sheep. They march to the beat of the taskmaster's drum.

Wa-Lu: Like your father, Jesus. They keep working for the man and get nowhere. They never fully participate in life.

The Lessons of the Taoists

Jesus: Yes, and my father who is my step-father is luckier than my real father, who probably stood up to the Romans and paid a price that I shall never know about.

Wa-Lu: Does it have to be this way?

Jesus: Only a force greater than them can overcome this natural tendency.

Wa-Lu: Such a force does not exist if your God has given his children free will.

Jesus: That is not quite true Wa-Lu, we the compassionate out number the dispassionate ruler of the world who kills from a distance, who makes violence the will of the state. He does not speak for God. We speak for God.

Jesus (again): We must confront the bully not on his terms, but ours.

Wa-Lu: Words are easy, Jesus.

Jesus: The Jews have a religion that caved into the warlords. The warlords appropriated, no, I mean stole, the religion from its peacemaking founders. The Jews can't even see it - they are blind. I have come to give them sight. I have come to give them their lives back. I have come to liberate them from the bondage that shackles their minds: their own religion. Wa-Lu, you must give your life over to something more important than yourself. Then you will live. They must be reborn to a new life of abundance. The community of the compassionate outnumber the violent. They can refuse to cooperate with his schemes. They shall inherit the earth, Wa-Lu. The warlords will destroy the earth.

The Story of the Savior, Jesus of Nazareth

Wa-Lu: Jesus your ideas are from another level. Putting them into reality on this lower level is another thing.

Jesus: I want you to teach me more of healing. More of the masters. Then I must go. My insides burn with desire to be of service to my fellow human being.

Wa-Lu: Melchizedek would call you a "Son" of God. He would call you a "Savior" if you transform your ideas into reality.

Jesus: Somebody's got to do it.

Jesus must have sat in on fifty different operative procedures done by village doctors to alleviate mankind's physical pains and diseases. One who was compassionate had to remove themselves from the loving relationship of those they operated upon. It was not nice. More often than not their surgical procedures did not work. However, many people, when given the choice would let them go ahead, saying death would be better than my life now. So they learned. They learned the hard way. What they did was to map the procedures and results for future generations. Thus Wa-Lu's library flourished with all kinds of interesting things. Wa-Lu taught that if you avail yourself of this storehouse of knowledge, you have many minds working through your mind to solve life's problems. The Savior of society must pay his or her dues. They live out hope for people who are used by the Prince. The Prince held this level firmly in his grip. Jesus felt that the only solution was to bring society to a new level. The Prince would not go away, but the problem would change to one of management. Wa-Lu always said that in order to solve a problem you must become bigger than the problem. Make sure that the Prince's power is spread. The power of the people's community would off-set the Prince's ability to use violence for his ends. Violence to the mind was

The Lessons of the Taoists

even a bigger problem for Jesus and Wa-Lu. How do you teach rebirth to a downtrodden world? The task is not easy. It needs many saviors. But it could work. Faith is in making good ideas work.

One day Wa-Lu and Jesus sat in the shade of a tree in one of the many oases around the great deserts of China. Their horses were tethered and calm. The troubles of the world were far distant, but they both knew that this was just an oasis. The problems of the world awaited them.

Wa-Lu: Jesus, what do you think is the highest level obtainable by a person?

Jesus: In this world?

Wa-Lu: Are there others?

Jesus: Of course, you need but look up in to the starry sky at night in deep reflection. I can feel, I can hear. The entire Universe is alive, Wa-Lu, but we are here. Our job is here and now. You must come to terms with this.

Wa-Lu: I know, you confirm it for me.

Jesus: The highest level is that of the human spirit in communion with the Tao, with God or Yomanne`.

Jesus: The many are many for the glory of the Tao. The spirit which is creativity itself moves with the Tao harmonizing the one and the many. It imagines the future, as does the Tao. In communion we talk to God of the experience and we create the Kingdom of God together. Thus we have purpose. We must come down from these lofty heights and put the communion into reality - that's what lives are for. But in the Tao's wake are many mansions. The good die young. The in-

The Story of the Savior, Jesus of Nazareth

nocent are made prey by the Prince of the World. Yes, God's light shines on the good and the bad. We leave it up to God to sort out the justice that slips through our fingers.

Wa-Lu: You have been reading Lao-Tzu. You with your keen mind probably know Lao-Tzu better than I.

They both chuckle.

Jesus: When you flatter me I know you're setting me up for something.

Wa-Lu: How do you take Lao-Tzu?

Jesus: Everyone will have their own opinion. Mine is that we, the operatives of the world, mediate yin and yang. They only exist because we exist in a Universe that has hot and cold. This is hot and cold to us. We mediate the two poles to find what is comfortable between their extremes. It is the Way through the fog. We have been given the ability to solve problems. God's Kingdom provides us tools with which to perform the job.

Wa-Lu: (from memory)

What is in the end to be shrunken,
Begins by first being stretched out.
What is in the end to be weakened,
Begins by being first made strong.
What is in the end to be thrown down,
Begins by being first set on high.
What is in the end to be despoiled,
Begins by first being richly endowed
Herein is the subtle wisdom of life:
The soft and weak overcomes

The Lessons of the Taoists

the hard and strong.
Just as the fish must not leave the deeps,
So the ruler must not display his weapons.

Jesus: (smiling and also from memory)

Why did the ancients prize the Tao?
Is it not because by virtue of it he who seeks finds?
And the guilty are forgiven?
That is why it is such a treasure to the world.

Wa-Lu: (smiles, nodding approval to Jesus' choice of Lao-Tzu's writings and offers another for introspection.)

I have three Treasures which I hold
fast and watch over closely. The first is
Mercy, The Second if Frugality. The third
is not daring to be first in the world.
Because I am merciful, therefore I can be brave.
Because I am frugal therefore I can be
generous. Because I dare not be first
therefore I can be chief of all vessels.

Jesus: (not to be outdone by Wa-Lu, offers up this tidbit from his memory bank)

He who knows how to guide a ruler in
the path of the Tao
Does not try to override the world
with force of arms.
It is the nature of a military weapon
to turn against its wielder
Wherever armies are stationed, thorny bushes
grow.
After a Great War, bad years invariably

The Story of the Savior, Jesus of Nazareth

follow.
What you want is to protect efficiently your
own state,
But not to aim at self aggrandizement.
After you have attained your purpose,
You must not parade your success,
You must not boast of your ability,
You must not feel proud,
You must rather regret that you had not
been able to prevent the war.
You must never think of conquering others
by force.
For to be over-developed is to hasten decay
And this is against Tao,
And what is against Tao will soon
cease to be.

Wa-Lu: Jesus you teach me!

They drink the clear water from the oasis. They jump in and frolic in the luxury of water in an otherwise desolate area. They laugh and play. Their serious journey to save the world must be balanced by fun. While drying themselves off Wa-Lu questions Jesus.

Wa-Lu: Do you remember the four-fold pathway of the Buddha?

Jesus: (from memory)

1.) The Noble Truth of Suffering.
2.) The Noble Truth of the Cause of Suffering.
3.) The Noble Truth of the Cessation of Suffering.
4.) The Noble Truth of the path that leads to the Cessation of Suffering.

The Lessons of the Taoists

Wa-Lu: Jesus; There is a very old legend I want to tell you about.

Jesus: Which of your legends are not old?

They laugh.

Wa-Lu: It seems as if this emperor who had everything decided that even his concubines would be in his army. He had thousands of women that were his at his bidding. But all they wanted to do was have fun. One day he invited a military expert to visit him. The military expert, having reviewed the situation, consulted the Emperor. Mr. Emperor, if you empower me to rule over your military, it will be the finest in the world. The Emperor relented. Some months later, the Emperor noticed that his women's army was drilling to perfection. They were the best in battle he was told. He took his General aside. "You have made them into a disciplined fighting force, but I miss my two favorite wives. I want them back." "It is too late," said the military man. "When you turned your concubines over to me I knew how to solve the problem right away. Your concubines thought only of having fun until I gathered them all together. In front of all of them I beheaded your two favorite wives with my sword. I said to the others, 'this is what will happen to you, if you do not obey.' I never had a problem after that."

Jesus: From Sun-Tzu on the Art of War?

Wa-Lu: Yes, you must study the bad with the good. Emperors have found out that there are men who will commit any distasteful deed, if they thought that they were doing it for the State. It gives them a go ahead to play out in reality their only means to having power. They exact a heavy toll on society. Countless millions of innocents never had lives because of them. And they receive the glory and are called patriots because they are willing to send others to their deaths without blinking any eye.

Jesus: Perhaps the Emperor and his military advisors should fight the battles they want fought. That would cure them.

Wa-Lu: As you look back in history, Jesus, the problem with society has always come from the top.

Jesus: The top few lord it over the rest of the people in all societies. Yes, it is the natural way.

Wa-Lu: Can you believe in a God that wants it this way?

Jesus: Of course not, I believe in the God who wants the people liberated. At Qumran, we study the Sons of Light. We also study the Sons of Darkness. We have in our library the Rules of War handed down by the Levites. Sun Tzu attempts to give the rules of a righteous war. Where some glimmer of justice is maintained.

Wa-Lu: In reality, there is no justice in war, Jesus. You win the war by whatever means available. Then, if the war is won you can talk of justice.

Jesus: While you are on your way to the next war.

Wa-Lu: True.

Jesus: I have come to this place to make mankind new. To bring them to a new level. War is unacceptable if mankind

The Lessons of the Taoists

is to advance. They will say, "This is an advanced society. War is a thing of the past."

Wa-Lu: How can you change the way people are?

Jesus: They are taught by The Way, The Tao. They have given themselves over to something higher than themselves. The Tao brings them up.

Wa-Lu: While you are on your one year journey back to your home, I would like you to read from the works of Chung Tzu. Imagine yourself one who Chung Tzu would ask the question, "Can we not like little children experience the 'eternal now' and have fun while we play out its games of reality? When we do we give ourselves a reason to live. We give ourselves a glimpse of the Kingdom of God."

Jesus: I'll race you back to the village, Wa-Lu.

Wa-Lu: You're on.

The two men bolted from the serene setting, hopping upon their waiting Arabian horses for some fun. The horses knew the way. The youthful men hollered and screamed as they raced to the village that seemed impervious to the outside world.
When they arrived back at the village there were hundreds of people awaiting them. Wa-Lu had taken Jesus to the nearby oasis so that all the people from the neighboring villages had time to gather at Wa-Lu's village to prepare the celebration for Jesus and Mary's departure the next day. They all cheered as the two young men on their Arabian mounts road in to the village. Wa-Lu and Jesus were now in the midst of the smiling, happy people of the Takla maken Shomo. As they got down from their horses, children rushed up to hug them. These two

were looked upon as the keepers of society. Almost everyone loved and respected them. Almost. Even now in the back of the crowd were young men who were envious of them. They coveted the cheers for themselves. They wanted the rewards that society had to offer. They were already planning and scheming in their minds to gain the control that their very being told them they must have. They lusted for it. Now they were onlookers.

Mary: Jesus, Wa-Lu! We've been waiting so long for you! Where have you been?

Wa-Lu: We ran into a couple of cute young ladies from another village and asked them to join us for a ride in the countryside.

Mary: As I watch the children, you let Wa-Lu lead you astray. (Looking at Jesus and pinching him lightly on the cheek.)

She now reaches to pinch Wa-Lu on his cheek and they all burst out with laughter. Tomorrow will be soon enough for melancholy feelings. Today and tonight they will celebrate and have fun.

Chapter Eight
Initiation

Later that evening around a huge fire, all the elders of the villages gathered to honor Jesus and Mary. They had enjoyed an evening of festivities. There had been many cooks with their newest recipes for succulent dishes of vegetables, fruits, fish, and meats. Jesus greatly enjoyed the food. Mary preferred her food more lightly spiced than did Jesus. Many of the men drank intoxicating juices and ate plants that made them a little light-headed. They knew from experience that this could become a problem with men. Not tonight, however. Tonight they were all happy.

At a certain point, after many songs and performances of villagers whose talents had previously gone unnoticed, they feel the warmth of the fire. They breathed in its smoke that smelled like mesquite. It was an enchanting moment in an enchanting land. Otherworldly, Mary thought. She luxuriated in the experience. Wa-Lu stands and bangs on a drum. The crowd hushes.

Wa-Lu: Tonight we honor our most beloved friends, Jesus and Mary from Jerusalem - one year's journey to the west. (Loud cheers go up and Wa-Lu waits for things to settle down and then bangs his drum. Everyone is silent again.)

Wa-Lu (again): I can't tell you how I will miss them (tears well up in Wa-Lu's eyes, as he knows the inevitable arrives tomorrow. He pauses and heads all droop.)

Wa-Lu (again): Our sorrow will become Jerusalem's joy. (The crowd all cheers again.)

The Story of the Savior, Jesus of Nazareth

Wa-Lu (After banging his drum.): Our wisest and most prosperous village elder, Ashkenazy, wishes to talk and then make a presentation to Jesus and Mary.

Wa-Lu beckons Ashkenazy from the crowd, where he sat with his five wives. Their children were sleeping and being taken care of by some of the younger women. Ashkenazy shuffled forward to the center area occupied by Wa-Lu. Jesus and Mary still sat on the ground. He embraced Wa-Lu. Ashkenazy had long light-brown hair and blue eyes. His skin was light olive and had no scratches or marks. He wore a garment of light colors that could be pulled over his head. One of his wives had made it for him. He wore leather shoes and dark flannel-type pants with straps over either shoulder that would button on the front. This was the way he kept his pants up. In addition, they were loose around the middle so that if he ate too much he wouldn't be uncomfortable. He wore a top hat with all kinds of bright and plumy bird feathers sewn in around its perimeter. He was clean-shaven. Ashkenazy had much land. He raised and trained horses. He had herds of donkeys, pigs and horses. He kept a herd of cows. He had built many buildings on his land. The villagers all loved him. He always took care of them. He always had jobs for them. He made sure that they didn't work too hard. He would join them in their work. He would not stay long at any one thing. He read manuscripts and copper sheets etched with writings. He gave much to the library that had been erected for all the villages. He built the library for the people. Everyone knew he was very learned. He now addresses the people.

Ashkenazy: Thank you, Wa-Lu. (Wa-Lu sits back down on the ground next to Mary and Jesus. They are just a few feet away from the "great man" and look up at him.)

Initiation

Ashkenazy (again): I too have come to love Mary and Jesus. Jesus worked for me training horses and teaching my children to ride. And better yet, to understand horses. Mary taught my children games. Her games taught children dexterity, having fun, and respecting one another. To the Far East, nearer to the unsurpassable ocean, dynasties with armies of war have arisen. The games the young men play there are games of war. For countless centuries the games have been made real.

I am getting old now. I have lived far longer than most. Some tribes who still measure age by the moon cycles would say that I am 540. By the cycle of the sun I am 45 years old. Other tribes measure age by methods only they could explain. I wish that all you young ones could have all the knowledge that I have in me, but at the age you are right now. Perhaps then you would not have to make all the mistakes that I made getting to where I am now. But then again, you might not understand the joy of discovery that is one of my greatest treasures.

The ancient Melchizedek said that those who are on a mission of discovery and share their findings with other people are on a higher plane of existence. Those who give to the future, to create a better future for everyone and make peace between tribes, are to be called the Sons of God. He called God Yomanne`.

Melchizedek was driven by an inner power. We do not know where this comes from. He traveled from the great ocean to the west to the great ocean to the east. All the land in-between was for everyone. Every person had the right to own, temporarily, a piece of it. He called this vast expanse of land the "Great Way." We are all brothers and sisters of the "Great Way." We all come from Yomanne`. Melchizedek said in his writings on copper sheets that he learned from those that came before him. He was a builder and built strong buildings. He was a builder of Cities of Peace, as were the line that came before him.

The Story of the Savior, Jesus of Nazareth

Some men did not agree with him. They used violence to impose their systems on people of peace. We have built a library here for all of the villages to share their common knowledge. It will be preserved for the future. The future must know of our mistakes. The future must know of our successes. Stored in our Library are recipes for making beer and wonderful mixtures of foods. There are treatises on growing grains. There are instructions on the keeping of herd animals. We depend on them for food and clothing. There are instructions on how to remove contaminations from inside another human being. There are instructions on the methods of celestial navigation. Not all the information is good. Although we live in peace here between a great desert and great mountains, we know that there are tribes in far off areas who fight against tribes. They build armies. The armies want to fight. Soon they fight to see who is better. The great desert and the great mountains have been our protectors.

Melchizedek became a wanderer in order to escape the lords of war. They would have him work for them. This he could not do lest he become like them. Arrogant and haughty were they. The Princes of the World were not for Melchizedek. I think of myself as a very fortunate man to be living here with you people of peace. Perhaps someday I will have to wander, too. Until then, I build libraries and schools for the children. I didn't make myself. The past made me. I have been able to survive due in large part to the knowledge handed down to me. You and I are different, yet we are one. We are at our best when we do not fight one another. Thank Yomanne` that we are different and thank Yomanne` that we are one. Jesus and Mary return tomorrow to Jerusalem. Melchizedek founded that city long ago. It was called Salem then. The city of peace. Melchizedek was known as the King of Peace.

Initiation

With that Ashkenazy asked Jesus and Mary to come forward. They approached Ashkenazy until they were only a few feet away.

Ashkenazy: (The crowd is silent. One hears the cracks and pops of the fire, as the wood becomes flame.) Jesus, Mary... I have known you both for quite some time. I know what burns in your heart young man. I know that Mary is here beside you to calm you and help you, and you her. You and she are one, just as you both and the Father are one. Would you please kneel before me as I commit you into the Order of Melchizedek?

Mary and Jesus both kneel.

Ashkenazy: (While placing one palm on Mary's forehead and one palm on Jesus' forehead.) I commit you both to the Order of Melchizedek. In the past the Sons of Darkness had made it unlawful. Will you both undertake to do your best to create your lives to the service of your fellows, your brothers, and your sisters, and to the betterment of Yomanne's world from whence you sprang and move and have your being? If so, answer "we will."

Mary: We will.

Jesus: We will.

Ashkenazy: (He now removes his hands from their foreheads and helps them arise. The crowd doesn't know whether to cheer yet, so they don't.) Jesus, you henceforth will be known to us as the Prince of Peace. You have ascended to a higher plane, and as you believe in your created mind, so shall you be.

The Story of the Savior, Jesus of Nazareth

Ashkenazy turns to Drashkar and grasps the copper sheet with ancient writings.

Ashkenazy: This was given to me by someone I hold dear. I give it to you. It is priceless beyond being bought or sold. These are etchings from the Savior, Melchizedek, in his own hand. He called his people "followers of the Way." They were not following him, they were following the Way. He showed them so that they might show others in the same spirit. The Way was brought down from Heaven. It was for all people to follow by their free will. If not, it was not from Heaven. The highest thing that you can give others is yourself, and until you lose yourself to them and Yomanne` you will not find yourself. You must create something of value to give them. You have done so, and now you and Mary go back to the world to give more.

Ashkenazy gives the priceless gift to Jesus. Jesus notices right away that the symbols it uses for letters and words and ideas are not dissimilar to those used in Aramaic or Chinese languages even though coming from the ancient past. Tears are streaming down Mary's face. She grasps for her braids and brings them forward to wipe the tears from her cheeks. The crowd erupts. The moment is sublime. The wood crackles and pops, as it becomes the flames, and the flames the smoke.

The next day Mary and Jesus loaded up all their belongings, and as many artifacts as they could, for the long journey home. Ak-Bar's son was the new caravan master. Wa-Lu and others hugged Mary and Jesus goodbye. Wa-Lu said that someday he hoped to come to their land. Away they went on the next leg of their journey.

Chapter Nine
Return to Qumran

One year later, a bedraggled pair of wanderers ride on horseback into Qumran. Levi began ringing the bell when he saw them coming. Anne, Aaron, and Isaac ran out to meet them. It had been six years. Surely it would take a week just to hear all the stories. When things had settled down, James and Jesus conversed over coffee by the fire in the Qumran Community Room.

James: Jesus, do you wish to continue your preparation, or has this long journey taken that out of you?

Jesus: I am more ready than ever. I now have a little confidence in me that was not there before.

James: Good! I have written a letter to an old friend in the masonry business who has made it big in Rome. He builds some of Rome's biggest and most important buildings.

Jesus: Mary will want to go.

James: I have anticipated this and have news for you.

Jesus: What is that?

James: Two energetic young men, Aaron and Isaac, have awaited your return for so long, Jesus. They remember how you would play games with them and take them into the countryside to learn. Lachesis said he would have jobs for them, too.

The Story of the Savior, Jesus of Nazareth

Jesus: Tell them to pack their bags. We leave soon.

When you are twenty-three or four years old everything is so much easier for you. The next horizon is not that far away. Jesus had a little ad-hoc family all of a sudden. The boys were very helpful. They were so happy to be on the adventure with Jesus and Mary, that they did things they would only grudgingly do at Qumran.

Rome was the next destination. They were grabbing life by the tail.

Chapter Ten
Rome

A few years have passed. Jesus walks up the steps of the Roman Government building with a determined look. It is summer and rather warm, so his hair is short and he is clean-shaven. His tunic does not quite reach the top of his knees. In his hand is a letter from the architect Lachesis Sinphonius, the man for whom Jesus works. He is a well-known and respected builder, often hired by the government to build their buildings. This letter would announce him to a government official and hopefully get Jesus a meeting with the Emperor. The letter read:

To Whom It May Concern:

The man who bears this letter is one Jesus of Nazareth who has been in my employ for almost six years. He is an apprentice architect and has built several of the government buildings here in Rome while under my direction and with my workers. He urgently desires a meeting with Senator Alvius Proximis with whom I have negotiated several transactions to build government buildings. He is a man of utmost character and integrity. I should be grateful if the good Senator would accommodate this request.

> *Rome Forever,*
> *Signed: Lachesis Sinphonius*
> *Architect of Rome*

Senator Proximis: Ah! Perhaps my friend will give us a better deal next time he bids a government job if I honor this letter? Yes, I will remind him (he keeps the letter and asks the attendant to escort this visitor to his chambers. A few minutes later the attendant returns with Jesus and knocks on the door of

The Story of the Savior, Jesus of Nazareth

the Senator's chambers.)

Attendant: Senator Proximis, Senator Proximis.

Senator Proximis: Show him in, Show him in.

The attendant opens the door and escorts Jesus into the Senator's messy chambers. Documents are scattered all over the place. His windows are open to keep the place ventilated. It is mid-morning. It's not yet unbearably hot.

Senator Proximis: Young man, you work for a friend. A tough negotiator, but one of Rome's best builders. If the Emperor wasn't so busy, he might be persuading Lachesis Sinphonius to work for him. What brings you here to me?

Jesus: I urgently desire a hearing with the Emperor.

Senator Proximis (half laughingly): The Emperor Tiberias has moved his royal throne to the Isle of Capri. He sees no one except who he wants to see, which is hardly anyone. He rules by writing letters.

Jesus: I would travel there to meet with him. Would you please write to him and ask him? I do no harm to anyone.

Senator Proximis: What is the nature of your visit? May I tell His Excellency of your cause?

Jesus: I come from Jerusalem in Palestine, a Roman Protectorate. There is much unrest there amongst the people.

Rome

Senator Proximis: Ha! If you only knew. We have complaints from all over the Empire. This is nothing new.

Jesus: This is different. There may be needless bloodshed. The Jews and the Arabs are restless. They get taxed heavily by the State and have nothing to show for it.

Senator Proximis: You don't know, nor do they, how fortunate they are. We protect them from the Barbarians all around the edges of the Empire.

Jesus: It does you no good to have an Empire where the people are not happy. They lead hard lives.

Senator Proximis: What is so bad about their lives?

Jesus: They work, work, and work. That's all they do. For what? Then they get drunk and sleep until its time to work again.

Senator Proximis: Don't you recognize stability? If they were not like this, they would be fighting one another - over who knows what. The Emperors have always recognized that stability of the masses is necessary for the good of the Empire.

Jesus: The Roman troops in Jerusalem take liberties with the women, both Jews and Arabs.

Senator Proximis: Come now. How old are you? Don't you know that boys will be boys? I am sure the Prefect in Jerusalem and the Governor of the province are well aware of what is going on. Once in a while you are bound to have some minor trouble, but you must think positively. These poor ignorants would be slaves to Barbarians if it were not for us Romans.

The Story of the Savior, Jesus of Nazareth

Senator Proximis thinks this young man has not seen enough of the real world to understand how things are. He will change, become hardened, thinks the Senator.

Jesus: I am afraid there is going to be violence that could be avoided by taking certain actions now.

Senator Proximis: I tell you what you should do. You write this letter, but do not make it too long or you will lose the Emperor. He wants things to the point, no beating around the bush. Bring it to me. I will see that it gets to the Emperor on his island.

Senator Proximis walks over to Jesus who gets up from his chair. Senator Proximis walks him out with his arm around Jesus' shoulder.

Senator Proximis: We need intelligent concerned young men like you in the Empire. Have you considered working for the State here in Rome?

Jesus: My mandate is to return soon to my people and help them grow out of their misery.

Senator Proximis: Yes, but just think what you could accomplish if you set your sights higher?

Jesus: I know what I must do.

Senator Proximis: What buildings have you been working on for the government?

Jesus: The new Justice Department Building.

Rome

Senator Proximis: Ah! The people of Rome clamor for speedy justice. Why do people always try to take advantage of one another? We would not need the judges. We could be building them another stadium for gladiator battles. The people perpetually bring claims against one another to be enforced by the state.

As Jesus walked down the steps he had mixed emotions. On the one hand, he had not accomplished his self-imposed mission - to be heard by the Emperor. But this was better than nothing.

Jesus: (turning back to speak) Senator how shall I address the Emperor?

Senator Proximis: You leave that to me.

LATER THAT EVENING

Jesus: Mary go get Aaron and Isaac. I have good news to talk about.

Mary goes out the door of their living quarters and heads for the stables. She found Isaac and Aaron there, caring for their Arabian horses. They were excited to hear what Jesus had found out.

Mary: Jesus, the boys will be here soon. I found them at the stables.

Aaron and Isaac appear in the room.

Jesus: Listen everyone, I met today with an important Senator from the government. He says that the Emperor has moved his residence to an island off the coast.

The Story of the Savior, Jesus of Nazareth

Jesus is seated at the table and is already writing.

Jesus (again): So I cannot see him, but I will be able to get a letter to him through Senator Proximis. It is to be short, but informative.

Isaac and Aaron offer help.

Jesus: You can help me by making as many copies of the letter as you can. When we go back to Jerusalem, we can show what we have communicated to the Emperor.

The letter:

My friends and I are here working in Rome building new buildings. We work for the leading architect of Rome, Lachesis Sinphonius. We currently are building the Department of Justice building. This brings me to my point. As an apprentice builder, I learned much of the world. When a boy of fifteen, I was fortunate to work as a laborer in Jerusalem, building and repairing mostly, Roman buildings near Nazareth. One Spring, I traveled to Damascus and got a job with the best caravan master in the business. I traveled the "Silk Road" to China. While in China, I again worked as an apprentice builder. More importantly, during the four years that I resided in China, I was able to study the great wisdom of the Masters. The Buddha and Lao-Tzu. I also, studied Chung Tzu and Sun Tzu. They all learned from the Order of Melchizedek.
    A good builder knows that a building must have a firm foundation if it is to last and serve its inhabitants well. The Masters knew that the foundation of society must be secure and maintained. The leaders of society come from the masses or they come from the ruling class. Either way, when they come to power, they seem to forget the people and rule by authority. Their own power seems to become more important than the welfare of everyone.
    The Masters taught that when the few dominate the many and lead lives of wealth and arrogance, it inevitably brings discontent among the masses. The Masters taught that, since the ancient Mel-

Rome

chizedek, the history of the world has been warfare - going from one war to the next.

There is much discontent in Jerusalem. I warn you of this. It could be diffused, but if anything, it is being promoted. The wealthy Romans lead lives independent of the Arab and Hebrew citizens. They flaunt their wealth while the poor citizens work like animals. The Roman soldiers have been known to take liberties with the Arab and Hebrew women. We ask that they be reprimanded by the Roman Prefect. He says he reports the incidents to the government and the army, but nothing seems to change. Meanwhile the tax collector asks for more money from the poor people. Young Arab and Hebrew males talk about countermeasures. I learned guerilla warfare from the writings of Sun Tzu. I do not advocate it. Many do.

Melchizedek, who is more ancient than the Hebrews, has taught that Peacemaking is the Way of Society and that it is a continuous job. Its purpose is to diffuse trouble that leads to war. Peacemaking is at the very bottom of society. The poor, the hungry, the restless, the ignorant, the weak - Melchizedek walked with these people and healed them. He never, ever left them. He was a builder of buildings and a builder of society. The superior helps the inferior.

The Roman Prefect isolates himself. He has made a compact with higher-ups in the Hebrew religion. They lord it over the people. Authority and coercion permeate the air of Jerusalem. There are Roman soldiers everywhere. The Prefect talks of aqueducts and roads. When he builds something, he uses slaves or pays the Hebrew and Arab workers so little and expects such long hours that they lead miserable existences. On Saturdays, he throws out a few coins to the scrambling beggars from his balcony. They do not need money, they need lives. They need help from the superior. Then when they become superior they will help the inferior. You would not have insurrections.

I feel confident that you as Emperor of the mightiest Empire of all would want your people to enjoy life, to find happiness. This is why I so earnestly write this letter. I cannot do it alone. You must pay the people maintaining the foundation of society at least as much as the ones maintaining the top. You need an army at the bottom. An army of teachers and healers who live with the people. Everything is the reverse of the way it should be. There should be few left at the bottom and many on top.

The Story of the Savior, Jesus of Nazareth

Please give me the tools I need to help bring this about. I do not seek your throne. I am but a humble servant of mankind.

Your friend,
Jesus of Nazareth, from Palestine, a Protectorate of The Roman Empire.

Jesus: Read this letter, everybody.

Jesus motions to Mary, Aaron and Isaac. They stand over Jesus' shoulders around the table and read. Aaron speaks first.

Aaron: Jesus, you have great courage.

Jesus: Somebody has to. Nothing will change otherwise. You must change peoples' minds or they are lost.

Isaac: Maybe the Emperor does not want what you are asking.

Jesus: Then that is something even worse. If we do not find out, nothing will happen. Then, a different course of action should be taken.

Mary: I am afraid for your safety, Jesus. Why do you have to be like this? Can't we just go somewhere and get away from everything and have children?

Mary now has tears in her eyes and embraces her man. Destinies. Was this her destiny? To cry giant tears on the shoulder of the man she loved more than anything in the world. A love unconsummated, having no children. Perhaps the essence of her love was enough. Perhaps she had reached another plateau when she accepted that this would not be.

Rome

Now she was bigger than the problem. The problem had not gone away. It had changed form. Maybe this would make her life better. There was only one way to find out.

Mary (again): Come Jesus, get some sleep and I will go with you to deliver the letter in the morning.

The four adventurers in Rome would sleep. Their dreams are lost to the energy fields of the Cosmos. Their lives would challenge the Roman Empire to its core.

Chapter Eleven
Bread and Circuses

Already the streets of Rome are bustling with comings and goings. Horses with riders that have never been seen before and probably never will be again. For two people in their late twenties, these two had a wealth of knowledge packed into their heads. Nobody would have guessed. Then again, perhaps that sinister looking man over there is plotting something against the emperor. He shuffles away now into the shadows and the crowds. Beggars' voices are always heard. Some display talents or have some exotic animal that brings attention from a passerby. Occasionally a clink is heard. A small coin dropped in the cup held by an outstretched hand. The cup is a reminder that not everyone is born into circumstances that will lead to a "good" life.

Then there are the bathers. Rome and its surrounding villages are known for their bathhouses. If nothing else, these city dwellers were clean. Some bathhouses were good. Some were not so good. Then, too, it depended upon what time of day one went. Late at night you might see some sex. Lots of it. During the day, children and people getting out of the hot summer days. The bathhouses were communal activities and tended to reflect the hierarchical nature of Roman Society. Certain areas were for the upper crust. A donation to the upkeep of the system would result in an inscription and a special place for you and family. Running water was the key to keeping these places from stagnating. Running water is good, standing water bad. That's a rule of thumb. Roman engineers used their ingenuity to keep these places clean. They were gathering spots and the government knew it. Keeping the people entertained was a huge part of governance. Keeping them fed was another.

Bread and Circuses

The women learned to coyly show off for the men at the bathhouses. The children, of course, romped around in the nude all the time. There was a strange, unspoken, and different standard once they become teenagers. One end of the bathhouse was for men, the other end for women. The women would give the one they were trying to entice a peek now and then. Of course, that was hit or miss business because males they did not want were always looking for a peek too. The courtship rituals were endless, a constant shuffling of people to see who would suit whom. Some women got married and had children. Some women did not want children and would use a certain extract smeared inside the vagina to serve as a dam over which the sperm swimming upstream could not jump. The Roman sewage system depended on running water. The Emperor thought of the multitude as a bunch of unkempt animals. The bathhouses would be contaminated were it not for his Roman engineers taking care of his bathhouses.

The Emperors liked to take credit for what the people liked. They were experts on laying blame on someone else when the people snarled. The people wanted instant gratification. This is impossible. Therefore, a constant tension is set up between the state and the people. What is the voice of the people? More bathhouses, more free grain from northern Africa. Build bigger oar boats to ship it over the Great Sea (The Mediterranean) to Italy. More slaves to row. The Emperor wants no trouble in his home city. He would ride through the city streets in a gilded carriage, hoisted onto the shoulders of twenty or more slaves. The palace elite guard of Roman Police surrounded them. No errant knife from the crowd of the low life would reach the Emperor on these junkets. He would toss out gold coins with his inscription. The sweaty, stinking masses would wave and cheer. Fights would erupt for the coins. Behind this entourage was another. There were horse drawn carriages and wagons from the Emperors stables. They bore the Emperor's symbols of power. Inside, police scooped out free

The Story of the Savior, Jesus of Nazareth

grain to the people, who would hold aloft various receptacles to capture as many of the little seeds of life as they could.

Mary would not go to the Stadium with Jesus, Aaron, and Isaac. She would listen only to the stories of the chariot races. The Stadium was packed with people. The Emperor, or a high-ranking official, is always present in the prime viewing location - the Emperor's box. The contestants would start out in front of the cheering throng. Then, they would go over to the Emperors box and bow to whatever symbol of authority happened to be present. Bowing to the idea of some "superiority" was natural. The superior lorded over the inferior in the Roman world. The Roman world of superiority and inferiority was based upon violence.

Jesus was absolutely disgusted by his trip to the Stadium with Isaac and Aaron. A representative of the Emperor's Throne was there. It was a beautiful sunlit afternoon. Had he been in China, he may have gone on a horse ride of discovery with Mary. Perhaps a visit to a neighboring village to share delicate morsels of vegetables and meat, cooked over an open fire. At home in Galilee, he would have been out on the sea fishing or swimming with friends - not so in cosmopolitan Rome. In Rome, that day the gladiator lay prostrate beneath the sword point of his adversary. His first loss, and his last. Life or death? The gladiator quizzically looked up to the Emperor's box. The Emperor's man advised the dignitaries that they must make the decision. A wife of one accepted the challenge. She stood. Thumbs down. The crowd roared as the formerly undefeated gladiator was disemboweled before the bloodthirsty crowd. He writhed in agony for a short time, then died. He was hauled out feet-first, intestine's dragging in the dirt. Perhaps he would be fed to the dogs. Somehow these men had become convinced that dying for the Emperor was honorable. Others, former slaves, had nothing to lose. Win five matches in a row and you are a free man, with some gold coins in your pocket to boot. Dying in front of a ruthless mob was

Bread and Circuses

better than being a slave the rest of your depressing life. It also made for competitive matches.

The Roman masses demanded to be entertained. Life in the city was different from life in the country. The city dweller's class structure was immediately apparent. The best bathhouses were donated by some rich builder of aqueducts who had found his niche within the Emperor's power structure. He kept tabs on who was in and who was out. A well placed little gift of thanks here and there to the ones who had the power was rewarded in turn with valuable contracts. These could be agreements to provide low cost labor, from perhaps prisoners of war or the continuous stream of anti-social males working their way out of jail. The Emperor's sword was the most powerful symbol in the kingdom, next was money. The most prized women gravitated to the ones who could take care of them. Childlike romps with the common boys in bathhouses gave way to more mature romps in the bathhouses with the elite of Rome. Many women knew of herbs to keep themselves from getting pregnant. Then there was abortion. Many beautiful young women died from infections caused by crude abortions. Was it worth the risk? In Roman society, it was perhaps a greater risk to be one of the masses, when faces change from minute to minute. Would you rather be raped by Roman soldiers or police on their drunken night out? At least the bathhouses offered some modicum of respect.

The entertainment of the masses revolved around sex and violence. The two powers were materialized in the form of the sword and the Roman coin with the Emperor's face, reminding you of that power as you traded it for wine or bread. Yes, the Emperor had discovered that if they were not kept busy, they would notice how miserable they were. They would complain. "We need this, we need that." Most Emperors could not stay in Rome for long. The masses would drive them crazy. The Emperor made trade-offs with the elite to do this job. The Emperor would insure them of the proper police sup-

The Story of the Savior, Jesus of Nazareth

port to keep the masses from erupting. There was a seesaw battle. The Emperor needed huge sums to finance his wars. Growth was the objective. Growth of the protective perimeter of the Empire. It had not reached its boundary. Seek and destroy, then Romanize. The Emperors target? Security. For what? That was the next problem. Meanwhile the Emperor did not have to think about that. He would put that off. Let the Senators figure it out. Those backbiting politicians will take forever. Let the people yell and scream at them. The Emperor was treated to royal parades when he was around. Winner of battles. Now the people were safe to get drunk and bathe, then go to the Stadium for the latest extravaganza. Of course within this labyrinth of human society there were cracks where one might find a fulfilling life. The life of an artisan who took pride and pleasure in their trade or trades. A small family perhaps. Trips to the countryside or the sea. Beauty struggled to break free of its underpinnings. When going on a journey, one starts at the beginning. The art of the culture was captive to the baser elements. Perhaps its struggle for liberation would touch the minds of the people someday.

Chapter Twelve
Sejanus

Jesus pushed his way toward the government building. The other three were in line behind him. Up the steps, into the atrium, and back to the Senator's chambers. The guard announced their presence. Soon the four were escorted in.

Senator Proximis: If it is not my young friend from Jerusalem! With friends?

Jesus: Yes, Senator, these are my friends Mary, Aaron, and Isaac.

Mary: I am a rather special friend.

Senator Proximis (smiling): He has exquisite taste. I see you have a letter for me.

Jesus: Yes, for you to get to the Emperor. I earnestly desire a meeting with him. I will travel to Capri at his bidding.

Senator Proximis: First things first, my impetuous young man. Things do not work that easily around here. It may take me some time.

Jesus: How much time?

Senator Proximis: Why don't you check back with me in two weeks? Then I will have a clearer idea.

The Story of the Savior, Jesus of Nazareth

Jesus: Why two weeks? This is urgent. Many lives, of both Romans and the people of Palestine, are at risk.

Senator Proximis: Now, do not get too pushy with me or I will not help you at all!

Mary puts her hand on Jesus shoulder.

Mary: We must be going now, Jesus - you and the boys must be working soon.

Senator Proximis walks them back to the Atrium. They head back to the building of government buildings. The Senator heads back to his chambers. On his way back through the maze of sculptures, a handsome, state of the art "youngish looking" middle-age man approached him from an adjoining hallway.

Senator Proximis: Sejanus, nice to see you.

The two men clasped each other, with both hands firmly grasping the outside shoulders of the other. Sejanus was the captain of the elite palace guard. The best of the best. His job was security of the government. There were no threats from barbarians within the palace walls. However, there were threats from the barbarians working beside the Emperor, not to mention the barbarians in the provinces - who were used more than appreciated. Force, the ruler of the Roman world, was the extrapolated power from individuated minds that had no idea the dilemma they were in. War, revolution, war, revolution. Sejanus was one-half of the de facto Emperor team in Rome. Tiberias knew that his longevity was only secure in seclusion. With things quiet on the perimeter of the Empire, it would be the interior's turn to vent their anger at the overlords. Sejanus was a cool-handed killer. Tiberias placed him where he was

Sejanus

because Tiberias knew that Sejanus, given the power, could keep things in order for a while. Senator Proximis could do his best to keep the politicians arguing but going nowhere. In the meantime Tiberias could have as nice life as possible on Capri.

Sejanus: Who was that, Senator?

Senator Proximis: Oh! Just an impetuous young man, working here in Rome on government building programs.

Sejanus: He gave you a letter?

Senator Proximis: Yes, he wants a meeting with the Emperor?

Sejanus starts uncontrollably laughing. Senator Proximis cannot help laughing too.

Sejanus: The Emperor might try to make love to him. Would he want that?

Senator Proximis: No, he is not that type. He wants to save Jerusalem.

Sejanus: What is there to save?

Senator Proximis: I do not know. It's one of the squabbles going on in various parts of the Empire. We send those budding young stars of yours to be Prefects. The Governors of the provinces are usually too busy with the good life to pay any attention to the people.

Sejanus: Here, let me read that letter.

Sejanus grabs it out of the Senator's hands before the

The Story of the Savior, Jesus of Nazareth

Senator has time to offer it to Sejanus. He reads the letter.

Sejanus: I could use a smart young man like this in Rome. It's nice to see someone with motivation around here.

Senator Proximis: Most are afraid to be motivated, lest what they accomplish may get them killed.

Sejanus: I know well what you mean, Senator. Some of those greedy bastards working with you in the Senate have no scruples. They always look to increase their power at the expense of someone else. It's a wonder we still have an Empire.

Senator Proximis: The army, Sejanus. It's the army.

Sejanus: Tiberias knows how to keep the generals happy.

Senator Proximis: That's why he is on the Isle of Capri and we are here. He has made deals with each one of them, I am sure. When he dies, everybody else can fight over the Empire. In the meantime he is meditating in one of his gardens.

Sejanus: Well, it's not a bad deal for us, Senator.

Senator Proximis: I should say not, if we could just keep the lid on the pot.

Sejanus: Tiberias says give them water, sanitation, free grain from Egypt once in a while, clean bathhouses and frequent extravaganzas at the Stadium, and they will be happy.

Senator Proximis: Yes, but of course with help from your police force.

Sejanus

Sejanus: We pay them top wages. We have the best, and I expect a quiet city. They strike the fear of God in those who would break our laws.

Sejanus (again): There is no way Tiberias will see him, but I would like to speak with this Jesus. I could use him.

Senator Proximis: He is easy to find. He's working on the new government building with the architect Lachesis Sinphonius next to the Great Hall of Wars.

Sejanus: I think I shall send two of my men there tomorrow to fetch him.

THE NEXT MORNING

Jesus and Lachesis are standing on the street with a roll of papyrus. Each man holds an end with both hands and faces one another as they look at the plans. Just then, two highly decorated Roman Police saunter up to the two architects. Behind them is a horse drawn carriage driven by another policeman.

Policeman: Is this the new Hall of Justice that is being built?

Lachesis: Yes, I am the head architect and builder.

Policeman: Do you know of a Jesus from Nazareth in Palestine?

Jesus: I am he. (Jesus speaks somewhat nervously.)

Policeman: Sir, Sejanus would like to see you in his chambers at the government building.

The Story of the Savior, Jesus of Nazareth

Jesus: When?

Policeman: Now!

Lachesis (putting his arm around Jesus shoulder): Jesus, Sejanus is the most powerful man in Rome right now. He is the Emperor's Captain of the Palace Guard and Rome's Police. You would best respect his wishes.

Jesus: How would I get there?

Policeman: We have with us one of Sejanus' personal carriages. The driver will follow us as we escort you.

Jesus, never one to turn down an adventure, was cautious. He just did not want to be dumb about his choices. He looked at Lachesis. Lachesis nodded his approval with at least a small smile. Jesus hopped in. He yelled out the open window, "Lachesis, tell Aaron and Isaac about this. They should tell Mary not to worry." Lachesis nodded again, and off Jesus went to meet Rome's current most powerful and prestigious figure.
Jesus' mind is spinning. The Senator must have told him about me. Maybe this man could get me to the Emperor. I hope this is not danger - perhaps they think I am an assassin paid to kill the Emperor. I must go through with this. Perhaps we can once again bring Jerusalem back to being "The City of Peace."
This time they do not go in by the front door. There are myriads of stables behind the building with many carriages of different types scattered around. Men are working on the carriages; other horse trainers are walking horses around, all beautiful Arabians, undoubtedly the finest. Jesus, the "horseman," was in his element here.

Sejanus

Policeman: Sir, come this way with us, we will escort you to Sejanus' chambers.

There were guards everywhere as they walked in the back entrance. They came to the end of a wide hall and a foreboding looking large door. The Policeman rapped on the door. The door opened. There stood Sejanus. He wore a white tunic with a short skirt covering one-half his thighs. His hair was trimmed rather short, but it was thick and black. His complexion was clean of blemishes. His nails had been manicured. He was clean-shaven. Jesus thought of him as quite handsome. He was well muscled. He even smelled good. A man "of power." From whence cometh his power?

Sejanus: Finally, I get to meet the man who wrote that interesting letter meant for Tiberias Caesar. I have also read his letter of introduction from the Architect Lachesis Sinphonius. You are Jesus.

Jesus (seeing all the maps and other papers): You appear to be a busy man, judging from your office and all these maps.

Sejanus: That I am, Jesus. It is my job to know every square inch of Rome. Every aqueduct, every spring, every sewer line, every bathhouse. I know where the most dangerous men are. I know which Senator is sleeping with which Senator's wife. I know which Senators are lovers of men, which are killers, and which are doves.

Jesus: With you to protect him, why has he gone to the Isle of Capri?

Sejanus: It isn't unusual. Emperors are strange. I cannot say that I have them figured out.

The Story of the Savior, Jesus of Nazareth

Sejanus motions Jesus to sit. He rings a bell and a servant appears. Sejanus asks the servant to bring bread, fruit, and coffee.

Sejanus (again): Tiberias never did spend much time in Rome. He spent most of his time near the perimeters of the Empire going from one war front to the next. I think he thought it justified his existence. He never really was involved in any battles until they were over. His greatest strength is his ability to keep people like me happy. He knows how to satisfy his generals and keep them apart. And to keep them away from Rome. There are no wars at the moment. Unless he discovers a whole new part of the world to conquer, he must come back to Rome and govern. He, of course, has no idea how to govern. He is a man who has risen to his greatest level of ineptitude. Capri is escape for him. The Empire will govern itself. He left me with the job of being the iron fist of security, and Senator Proximis with the job of playing politics. Meanwhile Tiberias is going to do what is very difficult for a Roman Emperor.

Jesus: What is that?

Sejanus: Stay alive and attempt to enjoy life.

Jesus: Everyone thinks that the Emperor, being the most important man in the world, would have no problems.

Sejanus: When in Rome he sleeps in the most comfortable surroundings possible. Yet, I as his protector, hear the screams from his nightmares every night. I enter his chambers because it is my duty. He curls up like a little baby with sweat dripping from his forehead. He cannot allow his wife or concubines to sleep with him. He is so embarrassed by his nightmares.

Sejanus

Jesus: His power has not treated him kindly.

Sejanus: He dreams of being eaten alive by animals. How would you feel?

Jesus: Not good.

Sejanus: You waste your time wanting to talk to him. He is on Capri to avoid responsibility. He may well agree with everything you say in your letter, but he would never do anything about any of it. He wants to live a long life. What for I do not know. To me, he's never had a life and never will.

Jesus: What shall I do now? Can Senator Proximis help me? Can you help me?

Sejanus: Let's finish our lunch. I have horses waiting for us at the stables. I want to take you on a tour.

Even though Jesus was not getting very far with his idea, he found this whole thing fascinating. Many times you assume things to be true that are not. You must be careful with your assumptions.

His wish to see and talk to Tiberias may be full of honor and all well and good. The practical prospects of this actually happening seemed dim. A fantasy. Reality is not so easy. Talking out the Palestinian's problems with Tiberias did not seem to be a high priority with anybody. The poor people of his country - Africans, Arabs, and Jews seemed destined for the Roman solution. What was the Roman solution?
Did they even know how big a problem existed? Maybe things would get better. Surely some of these Romans must have compassion to try to help those that were not as fortunate as they? Would they try to keep their dominance over the earth

The Story of the Savior, Jesus of Nazareth

that had been won piece by piece by their ancestors, and even make it grow until all the peoples of the world were under their thumb? They then could call everyone free. Everyone free to do it their way, that is. The power seemed to linger with their system. The power of dominance by force. A new set of characters would act out the same play over and over. Jesus' education had revealed that the world had been this way since Moses. One had to go way back to the patriarchs and the ancient peacemaker Melchizedek before one found a different way. The Tao, the Great Way - The WAY had somehow been lost to the Gods of war. This the new Jews called the Devil. They envisioned him half-animal with horns, a scarlet color (the color of blood), and a pitchfork in hand to skewer the innocent. He was lustful. Some saw him as arrogant and a braggart. The Chinese saw him as the "Prince of the World." The top dog who ordered everyone else around. He took a short cut to superiority. His was false superiority. He bragged of battles won. The dead were the innocent, not him. He had found the magic elixir of the world - power.

Unfortunately, it was not the power of love and compassion. It was the power of fear. He could control the outcome through fear. Never mind the long-term consequences. Someone else could worry about that. Right now, right here, he could get results and get them fast. People caved in to him. When he was stabbed in the back, the stabber replaced him. Short term gain, long term pain. Melchizedek had saved the world once. Could it be saved again after countless centuries of warfare? The Chinese dynasties imperiled China. The Roman Empire imperiled the west. Would there be one huge conflagration where the innocents of the world fought and died, and a Prince emerged who would be replaced over and over and over? A rule of the sword where the people starved and supported the elite with the toil and sweat of dumbed down existence? Where the elite, rather than building up the base of society, neglected it? It certainly seemed headed that way for all

Sejanus

Jesus could see. The ancient Melchizedek talked of the rebirth of all humanity. He acted out peacemaking in his life. Jesus saw in the writing of Isaiah the cry for a new Savior to teach the world. Was this naive? Why not just cozy up to the system and have as good a life as possible? You cannot do anything about the unwritten system of the World. The Law. What was the Law? The Great Buddha saw the Law as freeing mankind. The system used the Law to impose a greater degree of control on the people. No, it went further. Man could not be saved by the Law. Mankind must be reborn. All you had to do was think about it. Jesus thought about it all the time. The rebirth was in the mind. It was expressed in the action of life. How do you act out rebirth on the stage of life? A daunting question.

At the stables.

Sejanus: Jesus, I hope this Arabian stallion is not too spirited for you. He is one of my favorites. "Black Beauty," I call him.

The horse snorted as the two men approached.

Jesus: We shall see, Sejanus.

Jesus confidently took the rein and stood next to the most beautiful horse he had ever seen. He talked slowly and soothingly to the horse while patting lightly his neck. He asked the horse to be his partner on their little adventure and hugged him around the neck. He hopped confidently upon the horse's back, which was draped with a small blanket. The horse graciously accepted its rider as if to say, "Show me the Way."

Sejanus: Aha, I see you have no trouble at all. Where did you learn the art?

The Story of the Savior, Jesus of Nazareth

Jesus almost slipped and said Qumran.

Jesus (haltingly): On the "Silk Road."

Sejanus: The "Silk Road"?

Jesus: Yes, the way to China. In China I taught horsemanship. Chinese horses are good for work and war, but not so good for riding. We in the west have the finest stocks of horses. They have the best camels. Their stock of Arabians is growing.

Sejanus was amazed at how much this young man knew. The average Roman of his age was bathing and getting drunk most of the time. Complaining about why the government was not giving them more to entertain their idle hours. The weekly blood baths at the Stadium were not enough.

Sejanus: I will take you on a tour of our lovely hills and show you a place where you might live someday.

Off went the two horsemen, through the back streets of Rome and now up into the beautiful foothills over looking the City.

Jesus: These villas are unbelievable, Sejanus. Who lives in them?

Sejanus: Mostly the wealthy of Rome. The merchants. The big merchants, not the little shopkeepers. The ones who own ships. The ones who own caravans. The ones who make wine and bring in wine from other countries. High-ranking government officials, including many Senators, live up here in the villas. I myself have a lovely place.

Sejanus

Jesus: Were you born into this?

Sejanus: No, I fought my way in. I was born poor. I had something inside me that caused me to not accept my plight. I was tired of being bullied. I decided to make something of myself. (Sejanus started laughing. A deep masculine laugh.) No, Jesus, the poor life is not for me. I do not ever want to go back where I came from. You will see my villa later.

Chapter Thirteen
A Healing

As they passed a villa a man came running out the front door.

The Man: Help me please, my daughter is dying. Oh! It is you Sejanus.

Sejanus: Have you sent a slave to Rome for help?

The Man: Who knows when and if he will return? I do not know what to do.

Sejanus: I know nothing of healing methods.

Jesus: I do Sejanus. May I look at the girl?

The Man: Who is this Sejanus?

Sejanus: He is a man who traveled many years ago to the far distant east. He learned many healing treatments there.

The men dismounted the horses and tethered them to a railing. They hurried into the villa.

The Man: My daughter is twelve years old. We have lost two other children. My wife is hysterical. We have just this one left.

Jesus: May I touch and feel her?

A Healing

The Man (his arm around his hysterical wife): Of course. Does she have a chance to live?

Jesus: We will see.

Jesus noticed that she was in pain and held her stomach with her two hands, as if to keep it from erupting. She was sweating.

Jesus (to the man and his wife): Has she eaten anything unusual or perhaps spoiled?

The Wife: Not that we know.

Jesus: How long has she been this way?

The Man: Only since yesterday, but she has not felt well for several days. She has thrown up her food more than once.

Jesus talked to the girl, but she just moaned. He began feeling and pushing down around her little belly with both of his hands and fingers.

Jesus: She appears somewhat bloated to me. Does she normally look this way?

The Wife: No, she is bloated even though she vomits.

Jesus: Where does it hurt the most, little one?

The Little Girl: Right here (she moaned and reached with her right hand to the lower right quadrant of her stomach.

She moaned again.

The Story of the Savior, Jesus of Nazareth

Jesus, with his right hand, pushed in. He then let up on the pressure. When he did she moaned some more.

Jesus: Little one, when does it hurt more - when I push in, or let up?

He did it one more time. He pushed in on the area that she had led him to. Then after a few seconds he let up.

The Little Girl: When you let up it hurts even more.

Jesus (To the mother, father, and Sejanus): May I have a word with you?

They all retracted to the main living area, away from the child's bed.

Jesus: This one is not easy. You must understand that the art of healing is not a sure thing and that very few people are proficient at it. Your child may well die.

With that the mother sobbed uncontrollably.

The Wife: We have already lost two children before age ten. I will do anything to save this one.

The Man: We have just met you. How can I believe you?

Jesus: I will leave you now if you so wish or I will help you, but if you decide on my help, it is no guarantee that your child will live.

The man: What would you do to save her?

A Healing

Jesus: Based upon the symptoms that I see. I would have to remove what I believe to be the source of her problems. I have seen this done before in China and have assisted with the procedure.

The man and wife confer. Sejanus looks on in amazement at this whole episode.

The Man (to his wife): Perhaps we should do nothing and wait for the slave to return from Rome.

The Wife: Our last two children died without us doing much of anything, except for giving them some exotic herb that did not seem to help one bit. I look into this man's eyes and I trust him. We must take this chance.

The man (facing Jesus): I hope you know what you are doing. We feel as we must do something.

They look at the girl a few feet away as she continues writhing and holding her stomach.

Jesus: Please get me pots of boiling water. Two sharp knives, the softest cloths you have, and any stitching tools and threads you have for making clothes. We need either your strongest wine or the strongest hemp that you smoke. Preferably we need both.

A few minutes later they came back with all of the items.

Jesus instructed them to put the knives in the boiling water. He rolled some of the hemp into a couple of small balls. He then poured some wine into a pottery chalice. He had the little girl swallow the two balls of hemp with the aid of the wine.

The Story of the Savior, Jesus of Nazareth

Jesus asked the mother to stand by him. He intended to make a small cut in the lower right hand side of the girl's abdomen. There would be blood and the mother was to absorb it with the soft cloths. The mother could not bear to watch the procedure. Jesus waited a little while for the wine and cannabis to have effect. It is to be hoped that the little girl will not feel too much pain.

Jesus: There, I now have the cut I need. You, (talking to the mother) must absorb this blood with your cloths.

Jesus gently pulled apart the incision and gazed in. Sure enough, there attached to the base of the large tube-like gut, was a little two or three-inch long worm-like protrusion that appeared inflamed and swollen. With one quick flick of the knife he cut out the offender at its base, where it met the larger tube-like gut. He asked for the stitching tools and thread. He closed up the gut very promptly then stitched the skin together where he had made the cut.

The little girl was sleeping and appeared none the worse for wear.

Jesus: You must keep this wound very clean over the next few days. I suggest that you wash it with your strongest wine. Eventually the skin will grow together. If I have been correct in my procedure, she should live. Judging from what I saw, we got the problem, but one never knows. We are just learning about healing. Someday people will be able to do much more. They will learn from our successes and failures.

The mother held her child's hand and patted it gently. The father and Sejanus were awestruck.

A Healing

The Father: How can I repay you? What do I owe you?

Jesus: In this circumstance you owe me nothing.

The Father (to Sejanus): Sejanus, I will talk to you sometime later about this.

Sejanus: Yes, Senator, after I have talked more with Jesus. Now we must continue on our way. I have much more to show him.

The man and the woman thanked Jesus profusely. The two men mounted their Arabian stallions and rode off to the next stop. The next stop was Sejanus' villa near the top of the highest hill overlooking Rome.

Chapter Fourteen
The Lap of Luxury

Sejanus: I have two slaves who take care of my personal needs. (Just then one of them appeared.)

Slave #1: Master, Sejanus, and what can I do for you at this moment?

Sejanus: Put together some fruit, bread, and cheeses. Some wine and fruit juice. Where are my women?

Slave #1: They lounge by your pool.

Sejanus: Come with me Jesus, to meet three lovely ladies.

They walked out the back door of the villa into a beautiful garden with blooming flowers and smallish bushy trees that appeared to bear some sort of fruit. The fresh smells were enchanting. They walked through the garden to a good-sized pool. Three scantily clad young ladies waved at them from across the pool.

Sejanus: Power is intoxicating Jesus. When I was young and poor and had nothing, I always wondered about these villas and who lived in them. Now I know. I will never go back to the poor. I paid my dues. Now I deserve these lovely women. When, and if, I tire of them, I will get my pick of three or four more to replace them. Come, let us sit by the pool, my slave will bring us food.

The Lap of Luxury

The two men sat and Jesus noticed the statues around the pool. Statues of nude men and nude women staring blankly at their viewer. They had no feelings, no emotions. Had Sejanus been hurt so bad that he did not want to experience emotions anymore? Some men become callous after having been hurt or bullied.

Jesus: Sejanus, what is your role in the government?

Sejanus: With Tiberias gone, I am the enforcer. The palace guard and the police of Rome report to me. I am separate from the military. I have nothing to do with the generals. None of them are in Rome anyway. They report directly to Tiberias on Capri. He keeps the generals separated from the government. He is the master of controlling power. He does not know much about living. He is trapped in his world of playing one power against the next.

Jesus: How so?

Sejanus: Many Senators and the bureaucrats that run the government would like to do certain things to change the way things are run. They are sensitive to the needs of the people. Other Senators merely see their jobs as a reward for service to Tiberias. They inhabit the finest villas in the hills.

Jesus: But what about the elections by the people?

Sejanus: A sham. Tiberias finagles whom he wants. If they become too boisterous in their opposition to the established network of his, they somehow disappear. Tiberias calls upon me to do his dirty work in Rome. The generals do his dirty work at the perimeters of the Empire and in places within the far-flung Empire where rebels fight against Roman domination. He would never draw blood, but he holds ultimate power.

The Story of the Savior, Jesus of Nazareth

The innocents die at the hands of the likes of the generals and me. Order in the empire is paramount. Order only comes by the highest of authority. That authority is violence. I unlike, Tiberias, have no problem exercising authority on behalf of the state. I owe my very life to my ability to win over my competitors. I learned the hard way. Rather than die like my brothers, I learned to fight. I know all the ways there are to know about maintaining strict control over the dumb mobs. Tiberias thinks he must entertain them to win their approval, so that they will pay their taxes. He wants to be loved and admired. He will not do the dirty work. He pays me handsomely to take the burden from him. He knows he can count on me. If a Senator gets under his skin, I let that Senator know clearly the risks he takes. If they go too far, my men make them and their families disappear. We have been known to catch them trying to leave the Empire on caravans. We have spies everywhere. They headhunt for me. When caught, Tiberias' enemies are publicly dealt with as examples. We have ways of public torture. The price of resisting authority is high.

Jesus thought back to the incident not far from Damascus on the "Silk Road." Now he was face to face with the executioner. Who was the executioner? Tiberias? Sejanus? The Spy? The officers, on down the line to the soldiers, merely carrying out cold-blooded killings with no remorse. The soldiers did it because they were trained to. They did it for the State. Somehow this whole thing bothered him. Tiberias in seclusion, Sejanus and some purchased Senator running the government in Rome. The generals in the field with their little empires. It was empires within the Empire. Only a few enjoyed the villas. Tiberias had his island retreat and was oblivious to the masses. He had rationalized within himself that this is the way it works best. The alternative of anarchy was less preferable than ruling with the sharp blade of the sword. Sejanus said that maybe it has its faults, but it is the best system in the world.

The Lap of Luxury

Sejanus: Come now Jesus, I will take you to the very top of the hill not far from here and we will look down upon our subjects.

Off they went. Sejanus kissed his lovely ladies' goodbye. They would patiently await his return. They neared the top of the hill. Jesus first noticed the aqueducts, then the giant reservoirs. There were hundreds of workers up here managing the water source for the Romans.

Jesus: This is unbelievable. I have never seen such an operation!

Sejanus: I also run this operation. We have had workers, who are either slaves or prisoners of war, digging our reservoirs. We collect rainwater. We also have a constant stream of slaves with donkeys that bring up lots of fresh water from lakes below. Tiberias wants fresh water running at all times in the bathhouses in Rome. All the public officials supporting him have villas in the hills. They get the fresh water first. The fresh water also flows through our public sanitation system, to holding ponds away from the city. Tiberias, as well as Emperors before him, wanted Rome to be the center of the world's civilization. Tiberias is done expanding the Empire. He writes that future Emperors will eventually make the whole known world into one big Roman Empire.

Jesus: What is the difference between the prisoners of war and the slaves?

Sejanus: We must buy the slaves from slave traders. Most slaves are neutered and used for lighter jobs - like the household slaves at my villa. When neutered, they are not a threat to my women, but they do tend to get a little fat. They become rather passive. Rarely do they give their Roman masters trouble, and they tend to accept their lot in life and even enjoy it. Tiberias makes the generals give up twenty-five percent of their prisoners of war to work on government projects. We do not neuter them because we get more work out of them if they are not neutered. We have learned to feed them well, and learned how to get the most work out of them. The problem is that when we keep them healthy, some try to escape. We make a public show of captured runaways to discourage others. We have plenty of torture rituals that we make the other prisoners watch. It might take two or three days of agony for one of them to finally die. If they are hurt on the job so that they cannot work, we kill them mercifully and do not make a public spectacle of them. It has been an advancement over the past when the injured were kept working until they died. Under my leadership I think we take the best care of slaves and prisoners in the history of the Empire.

To Jesus this whole thing was revolting and more barbaric than the barbarians they imprisoned.

The Roman's motto was "do unto others before they did unto you." What force could oppose these stealers of people's lives? Where was their compassion? Where does this way of looking at the world come from? His friends at Qumran, and his friends in the peaceful villages of China, were not this way. They looked at the world differently. Why? How did it get this way? The words of Isaiah echoed over and over in his mind. The words of Lao-Tzu and the Buddha echoed over and over in his mind. It does not have to be this way. It should not be this way.

Sejanus: Jesus, I have noticed your talents. You have much that you could contribute to the Roman Empire. Come here to the Palace and work for me. One day you will have your own villa with slaves and all the women you want. The

The Lap of Laxara

people will recognize your power and will worship you. You might even become the Governor of a large province. You perhaps could be the ruler of Palestine. If you fall in line with the system, you will have rewards beyond your dreams. I am here to give you the opportunity of a lifetime.

Jesus glanced over to the right, where a couple of hundred yards away a soldier was whipping a slave. Jesus was revolted by Sejanus suggestion.

Jesus: Let me go back to my apartment in the back streets of Rome and think about it. I would also like to talk to my employer, Lachesis Sinphonius. We are in the midst of a large building project.

Sejanus: Do not worry about him. He would not dare complain to me. I will replace you with two or three if he so desires.

Jesus: I would rather leave him on good terms, Sejanus. Remember, he is one of the largest builders in Rome and for the government.

The ride back took too long for Jesus. It seemed like forever. There was no way that Jesus could give his life to the system. He wanted to change the system. The wrong men controlled it. They appropriated what and whom they wished and have some sort of unwritten alliance of power. No, it was not for him. They were his adversaries.

After their long day in the hills of Rome, Jesus and Sejanus talked as their horses were being attended by the stable boys. Sejanus has an idea to help entice Jesus to work for him in Rome.

The Story of the Savior, Jesus of Nazareth

Sejanus: Would you come to a gathering I will be hosting one week from today? Your employer, the mason, has already been invited. It will give you a good chance to meet some of the most influential people in the Empire. You could bring your friends too. Once they see how they could lead their lives, they might be good at influencing you.

Jesus: Hmm! I will talk to them to see...

Sejanus now interrupts Jesus.

Sejanus: I will have my best valet bring you back tonight so that he knows where to pick you and your friends up. They will escort you and the stone mason to the event.

Jesus now knows a little about Sejanus. What he wants done is what happens. He is in the habit of giving orders, not taking them.

LATER THAT EVENING

Later that evening, Jesus talks about the day's events with Mary, Isaac, and Aaron. The young men are fascinated listeners. Jesus has always been a good storyteller. They could listen to his stories for hours. He had paid the price. He had lots of stories to tell. Mary had always asked Jesus whether there was any way he could try to fix the "system" from the inside. They could be married, have children, and while she was busy with the young ones, he could be saving the world. He was always changing the subject. Maybe now was her chance to work on him.

Mary: You think its safe don't you, Jesus?

The Lap of Luxury

Jesus: We would be escorted by the law enforcer's best valets. I don't worry about your safety so much as I do about the safety of your minds.

Isaac: Jesus, this is an adventure for us. We want to have "brass balls" just like you.

Jesus: Wa-Lu would say that sometimes discretion is better than valor.

Aaron: Jesus, we came here to learn. How will we learn anything unless we take some chances?

Jesus: You are right. We will all go.

The next day Jesus talks with his employer, Lachesis the builder.

Lachesis: Jesus you will see what a corrupt bunch they are. I grew up in Gaul and was taught masonry by my father. Some of the finest structures were built there. Their purpose was to protect people from the crudest barbarians of them all, the Romans. They are the most boastful, backbiting people I know. I had to change my name when I took on a job in Italy. One thing led to another, and with Rome growing as fast as it is, my job became a business. The business has too much of me. Someday, I will return to Gaul with my wife. She is unable to bear children. She is my real life, and she is miserable here in Rome. The people think about showing off too much for her. Some time when I get a building done, and before they get a chance to stick me with another one, I will sneak off in the middle of the night.

Jesus: You are paid well aren't you, Lachesis?

The Story of the Savior, Jesus of Nazareth

Lachesis: What good does that do if you can't enjoy it?

Chapter Fifteen
The Lure of Money and Power

The scene shifts to the gala event the next week. Mary had made Roman-looking clothes for them. She cut and groomed the men's hair. They even dug out dirt from under their fingernails. They were clean-shaven. Their tunics were sparkling white. They all went to a Roman bathhouse to clean up. Mary had purchased some sweet-smelling oils in Rome. She wished she had some of her toiletries from China. Roman stuff would have to do. Mary always accused the men of smelling like the stables. Since Mary was going - Lachesis' wife Rene' agreed to go too.

The view of Rome from Sejanus' estate was breathtaking. It was summer, and not as hot in the hills as it was in city. Puffy white clouds drifted aimlessly above. They were far from the struggle of the masses. Harp players were stationed everywhere. The music was soothing. Fresh fruit and wine was everywhere. Some smoked hemp from pots that were passed around. Jesus thought that there were easily 300 people here, and the women outnumbered the men. Some admired the sculptures as they sipped their wine. Some were eating cheeses and breads and salted fish that looked like sardines. A few fat, balding men sat at pool edge with their feet in the water, probably talking about politics until some scantily clad young Roman or Greek girl walked by showing off to them. Sejanus introduced Jesus to Theros Marcion. He looked Greek and had the most beautiful silver, wavy hair that Jesus had ever seen. Mary and Rene' were thankfully occupied looking at the view and discussing all the artifacts so ostentatiously placed around the grounds. Aaron and Isaac were flirting with girls. Lachesis had pigeonholed a Roman Senator. They probably were talking about Rome's look of the future. After Sejanus made the introduction, he waved to someone a few feet away and left Jesus to fend for himself. Who was this person who stood before him?

Marcion: Thank you for asking young man. I own 26 ships that ply the Mediterranean. They bring wheat and Papyrus from North Africa to Italy. To the east they harbor in the safe Turkish ports awaiting the trading caravans coming back from the "Silk Road" that goes all the way to China. I buy low from them and get the goods to the ports in Greece and Italy where I sell high.

These caravans bring back untold treasures from the east. Silk clothing, spices, precious stones, hashish, and plants much stronger than hashish. They bring young women and boys that will be sold to the rich for their pleasures. It's a good business, but it drives me crazy sometimes.

Jesus: Why?

Marcion: I must please too many different people. The caravan masters have it made. They go off for 2 years sometimes, and don't get involved in all the politics around here. What do you do young man?

Jesus: I am an apprentice mason. (He points to Lachesis some 20 feet away.) Working for that man over there.

Marcion: You will never make much money being a mason.

Jesus: Why?

Marcion: I know them. They are too nice. I suppose he even pays you.

The Lure of Money and Power

Jesus: Yes, I would like to make more, but I realize I must pay my dues. How can you get good help any other way?

Marcion: You must learn to think like a Roman businessman. None of the stonemasons come from here. They have learned some foolish things somewhere.

Jesus knows he has a different kind of brain here. He must mine it to see how it thinks.

Jesus: How do you do it?

Marcion: What?

Jesus: Make a living in your business?

Marcion: For one thing, I'm not interested in "making a living" as you say it. I'm interested in being the richest man in the world. Someday my sons and their sons and their sons will control the trading in the world. Everyone wants to trade. The rich need something to do. They will buy anything that they can't get here. They like to show off their wealth.

Jesus: What are the biggest problems in your business?

Marcion: Finding cheap labor. To beat the competition in my business, I have learned not to rely on sails like the little guys. I have sails on my ships, of course, but I also have oarsman. The little guys can't buy very many slaves. They've become too expensive. Since that kook, Tiberias, withdrew to his stupid island, the generals are only working on inside trouble. We don't get many slaves from inside trouble. So I came up with an ingenious idea. I convinced Sejanus that to make these Roman "fat cats" happy, I needed an unimpeded flow of goods

The Story of the Savior, Jesus of Nazareth

coming into the eastern ports from the Silk Roads. Sejanus set me up with the eastern general Dios. He had one division in Turkey that was getting bored. Tiberias would never know, as Sejanus censored every piece of information that was sent to him. Besides Tiberias had become soft. He was tired of bloodshed. He was content with his gardens and young men. Somehow, he thought by making love to young men, he would make up for all the ones he had sent to their deaths before they even knew what was going on. Numbers - that's all they were to him.

Jesus: So what was your great idea?

Marcion: On the Silk Road the caravan masters were being robbed by bands of lawless hoodlums. Surely it would not take a whole Roman division to clean this mess up. I paid Sejanus and the general a gratuity from my business to help. Normally the generals would have their soldiers just go in to the small villages along the routes and kill a few of the young men in the public square. But I had a better idea. Bring them back to me and we would use them for rowers. It was a win-win for everyone.

Jesus: Except the young men.

Marcion: They had rotten, god-forsaken lives. I at least fed them and gave them discipline in their miserable, lawless lives.

Jesus: Could they leave your employ?

Marcion: Absolutely not. They were mine for life.

Jesus: Could they marry?

The Lure of Money and Power

Marcion: Surely you jest me. This is a tough brutal world we live in young man. They worked, ate, and slept. They were chained to one another. Every once in awhile one would make trouble. He would be given a very severe lesson in front of the others by one of his own, who was treated specially for cooperating with us. My only problem is a couple of these dumb-ass liberal Senators here in Rome, who hear reports and pick on me in order to get votes.

Jesus: Are they here?

Jesus thought that he might get their view of this ugly situation

Marcion: At Sejanus' gathering? (Marcion smirks) He wouldn't let them get near here. They don't live in the hills. They don't even know we're here today.

Jesus thinks to himself, "How can a man think this way? Why do I think so differently from him? I could never take someone's life from them no matter how I tried to justify it. Oh! I could probably do it in self-defense but I've never been tested. This was a different kind of taking someone's life. Was there no law against this? How could men be so cruel?" As Jesus ponders, Marcion waves to someone and leaves.

A voice: Jesus, is that you?

Jesus is jolted back to reality. He turns toward the voice. It is the father of the little girl who Jesus treated on his day in the hills with Sejanus. Jesus reaches out both of his hands to him.

Alerius: My name is Alerius - we were not properly introduced. I was in a daze. My wife Helene was in a daze.

The Story of the Savior, Jesus of Nazareth

(Alerius now pulls Jesus to him and embraces him.) My wife has not slept very much but our little girl, Cythios, is doing fine. My wife continually washes her wound with water to keep it clean.

Jesus: Fresh, clean water has healing powers. You living in the hills get the freshest water.

Alerius: I have talked to Sejanus about recompense for you. He says he thinks that you will go to work for him. I am a Senator and know the wealthiest people, not only here in Rome, but around the perimeter of the Great Sea. I will see to it that you will have one of the finest villas here in the hills. You will be able to have the "good life" that very few get to enjoy. You will pay nothing for it. It will be yours.

Jesus: I'm curious, you as a leading Senator, what are the biggest problems you face here in Rome?

Alerius: Satisfying the riff-raff. Law and order. We don't want them coming up here and stealing from us. Sejanus has an excellent police force but it takes other things.

Jesus: Like what?

Alerius: I can't name them all but we in the Senate talk about it all the time. The Stadium is very important. The chariot races. The gladiator battles. The slave/animal duels.

Jesus: The slave/animal duels?

Alerius: Yes, the slaves who do not accept their lot are used for entertainment of the bloodthirsty masses. They love to watch violence. We put them in against a pack of wolves or a lion. These animals haven't been fed for a couple of days.

The Lure of Money and Power

They rub goose-blood all over the slaves. The riff-raff make bets on how long the slaves will last. They are numbered and they go down to the holding cages for the slaves beforehand to see which ones look the strongest and will hold out the longest. If a slave makes it to the end, it pays more to the ones who picked him or her. Some slaves have been known to make it through 10 contests before they are devoured. They become legends. Humans can be quite resilient sometimes.

Jesus wanted to get off this grisly subject.

Jesus: What else do you do for them?

Alerius: Roads, aqueducts, temples, libraries, free grain, and maybe their favorite pastime - bathhouses. Tiberias said you have to keep them busy and somewhat satisfied or they will revolt. He doesn't mind revolts out in the provinces so much, but he doesn't want them in Rome.

Jesus: How come Tiberias isn't here?

Alerius: There are no big threats from outside the perimeter of the Empire now. He has tired of overseeing the slaughter of more people. He knows that the next battles will now be on the inside of the Empire. Men will fight with their own countrymen once they have no common outside threat that binds them together. They will argue to the death about how the country should be run. We in the hills want to conserve our hard-earned wealth. Some Senators who live with the riff-raff don't understand this because they've never been wealthy. We try our best to keep them out of the Senate, but we have been forced to keep some of them to avoid a revolt of the lower classes. So Tiberias doesn't want to get stabbed in the back. He wants to spend his last years in luxury and peace. He can get away with it because he has Sejanus, who would kill anyone at the drop of a hat and say he was doing it for the state. He doesn't know what guilt is. He conceals it from himself and meanwhile enjoys the power he never could have dreamt of when he was a young boy.

Jesus sees Mary beckoning to him.

Jesus: Alerius, I must join my lady friend. Would you please excuse me?

Alerius: Of course, But you must bring her to my villa soon so that I may meet her. We might all bathe together and become more intimate friends. My wife finds you attractive.

Jesus wants to get out of here in the worst way. He walks briskly towards Mary. He notices that the torches spaced around the pool enable him to see that many Senators and the elite of Rome's society are naked in the pool, frolicking with Sejanus' women and perhaps some of their friends. He doubted whether the other girls were wives of the dignitaries.

Mary: Jesus, I've found the most beautiful spot overlooking Rome. Come with me, it even has a marble bench that we can sit on.

Mary led Jesus up a little winding pathway through the lush vegetation. Wonderful smells of fresh flowers wafted through the air. They emerged from the vegetation to a clearing. There was the marble bench facing a spectacular view of the largest city in the Mediterranean world. Much bigger than Jerusalem. It was dark now and the stars twinkled overhead. A few feet ahead the terrain slanted downward. The lights from the city mesmerized the two world-travelers. Surely they have had experiences that very few of their age did. Jesus held Mary's hand and looked upward to the twinkling stars. He

The Lure of Money and Power

thanked the Father. He tingled inside with the glory of creation. They sat down on the bench.

Mary: Jesus, talk to me. I know when your mind needs to be unloaded.

Jesus: I feel thoughts before I can even verbalize them in my mind. We have been in Rome for some time now. We have been to their temples, their libraries. We see the way they live. Their libraries have nothing about the Buddha who came down from Heaven. They have nothing about the Great Tao or Lao-Tzu. No one has heard of Melchizedek, the "King of Righteousness." Our library at Qumran is full of the light these men shone on this dark world. I know this knowledge is coming back from the East. I think it is being censored from the people by the elite of the Roman Empire.

Mary: You could figure everything out, Jesus, if you were given enough time. Go on.

Jesus: I keep going over and over in my mind; what is the system they live by? They don't even know they are doing it. It keeps repeating itself with every generation. Ingrained is the dominance of the many by the few. The tool that is used is violence or coercion. Wars and revolutions have recurred throughout history. The periods of "rest" talked about in the Jewish Writings are few and far between. Joseph's good Pharaoh was replaced by a bad Pharaoh. Etched into the pleas of the Prophets is this very conundrum. Lao-Tzu was a Prophet. The Buddha was a Prophet. Isaiah was a Prophet who called for someone to save the world from this system based on violence. The bullies, more often than not, run the system. The revolutionaries who try to change it, most often become the bullies themselves once they have tasted power. Once in power they do not want to relinquish it. They seek more power. They

The Story of the Savior, Jesus of Nazareth

suppress the people and the cycle continues. Do you hear me, Mary, or is this too difficult to explain?

Mary: Women are second-class citizens. I have been propositioned tonight twice by two of Rome's drunken "leaders." Jesus, men are naturally this way. Unless they are taught about this and accept the need to change, they won't. You must start when they are children. Look at Isaac and Aaron; they were born selfish and ready to fight. Had we not taken them in, they would have either perished or fought their way through life.

Jesus: They teach nothing in their temples. Their "religion" as they call it is self- centered. They pray to Jupiter and Juno and I don't know how many other gods to give them what they want. If things are going good, it's the gods rewarding them. If things go bad, it is because the gods are unhappy with their behavior. Utter confusion about how to live their lives is the result, especially when they have these overwhelming animal-like drives compelling them. They sacrifice animals to the gods just as the High Priest of the Jews does. They cannot kill and burn enough animals. It is the animals within themselves that they must deal with.

Mary: Do you have any good ideas?

Jesus: I have dreams. The Jewish religion is like an old wineskin. The old wineskin is taut and cracked. When new wine is put in, it expands and bursts the wineskin. I would dare to combine the teaching of Lao-Tzu and the Buddha with the best of the Hebrew spiritual thoughts and teachings. They each compliment the other when understood. The salvational drive of Isaiah, I think, is deficient in the eastern body of spiritual thought. What burst through the wineskin would be called the WAY. We would look for saviors to teach and moti-

The Lure of Money and Power

vate to "save the World" - I could go on and on. Right now I think the most important thing is to gather up our friends and get out of here. Sejanus' fangs will not get me.

Mary and Jesus bid farewell to their beautiful view of Rome and its sea of lights. Then they went down the incline and back towards the world of the elite. Isaac, Aaron, Lachesis and Rene` were more than ready to leave. Sejanus by now was nowhere to be found. The number of drunken nudes in the pool had increased. The valets were sober. They escorted the group back to their homes in the lower elevations.

Chapter Sixteen
Return to Nazareth

Early the next morning Jesus was the first one at the jobsite. He must talk now with Lachesis. When Lachesis arrived they boiled some water and made coffee. Then they talked man to man.

Lachesis: I know you must go Jesus; you don't have to explain yourself to me. I live in a crack because of my knowledge of a very difficult trade. The Romans need me. We have an unwritten contract. Our tradesmen do not compete politically with them, but we have our own order. We do not give ourselves to their system. We are people of peace and harmony. Our order is secret.

Jesus: The Order of Melchizedek?

Lachesis: You amaze me.

Jesus: Back at Qumran in our library, I have some of his thoughts etched on a copper sheet. His thoughts were partially interpreted by Lao-Tzu and the Buddha. They are in my new body of spiritual thought. The ancients say that Melchizedek was not of an earthly lineage. I think he was, but his thoughts were so different, his way of living and leading his people so humble, that they thought he was unearthly. Mary and I were inducted into the Order in China.

Lachesis: You fear Sejanus, don't you?

Return to Nazareth

Jesus: He wants to use my talents for his own ends. I must get out of here before he impresses me into his service. I have no time for coercion. If actions do not come from free will, they are not from the Father in Heaven.

Lachesis: I have friends from the Order throughout the Empire. Go get your friends and what belongings you can loaded on your horses and come back here. I will make sure that you get back to your homes in Palestine safely. I cannot do anything about storms at sea, but I can make sure you get a good boat and a good sea captain.

Jesus embraced Lachesis. He mounted his horse and went to gather his family and head off on another adventure.

AWHILE LATER

Lachesis was good to his word. They rode to the nearest sailing port, and a talented sea captain sailed them to Caesarea Maritime. Their horses went with them. Back on horseback at Caesarea Maritime, in Palestine, they then headed east to Nazareth, where they stopped to visit Jesus' mother.

Jesus: Mother it is so good to see you! (They are in an embrace that seems as if it will last forever.)

Mary, Isaac, and Aaron watch as the two gaze at one another in disbelief.

Mary: Jesus, Jesus - I knew you would come back someday!

Jesus: I sent letters. Did they not get through?

Mary: I have two of them. I read them over and over.

The Story of the Savior, Jesus of Nazareth

Jesus: These are my friends, mother - Isaac, Aaron, and Mary.

The two Marys hug, then Mary the mother hugs Isaac and Aaron.

Mary (The Mother): Your three brothers are hard at work. They inherited a good business from your father. Yes, Jesus your father passed on some years ago. He worked himself to death. Your brothers toil under the same sun. They will be home tonight. They take care of me.

Jesus: I want to see them and spend some time here, but I must return to Qumran. I have decided to form a ministry in Jerusalem.

Mary (The Mother): A ministry? How will you make a living?

Jesus: The people are all working so hard that they never live. Someone must be here for them, to teach them how to live their own lives. It is being snatched from them in subtle ways. I don't worry where the money will come from. It will come from somewhere if I give them something of value.

They visited for a few days. Jesus' brothers even took a day off and Jesus took them fishing. Mary cooked the fish with some spices brought from China. She put olive oil on the chunks of fish and roasted them over the fire. Things felt so good now. How long can this feeling continue? The wanderer in Jesus prompted him to move on.

Jesus: Mother, I will be in Qumran for a while. Please don't tell anyone I am there. Then, when I establish my ministry, I will be able to see you more.

Return to Nazareth

They hugged goodbye and it was off to Qumran for the adventurers.

Chapter Seventeen
The Way

It is two days later at Qumran. James and Anne are told the adventurers were on their way. They were out in the field in the shade of a tree, waiting to greet them. Then, four people on horses appeared. Tears were streaming down Anne's face. They had been six years in Rome. Now they were back. What destinies awaited them all?

James: Aaron! Isaac!

James ran out further to greet them. Hugs from horseback don't work so well.

Jesus: We are finally back.

Jesus and Mary dismount. Young men from the stables have come forth to take care of the horses.

That evening after dinner, James, Jesus, Mary, and Anne sit and reminisce.

James: Are you any closer to "saving the world," Jesus?

Jesus: I think I know what must be done.

James: You are ahead of everyone else.

Jesus: The power of the Prince of the World must be blunted.

The Way

James: By whom?

Jesus: By the ones the Prince steps on to get to his throne.

James: There is no mechanism, and if the Emperors of the world knew about it, they would usurp it.

Jesus: Men and women are the same all over the world - that I have seen. In China, the family dynasties fight it out to see who will rule. Here in the West, Roman Emperors decide who will rule. They all rule by force.

James: This has gone on for millennia, Jesus.

Jesus: What the world needs, James, is a kinship of the masses. Unfortunately this does not happen naturally, it has to be purchased and then taught.

James: Purchased?

Jesus: They who enter through the Gate of Life will find it difficult. It is exhausting learning all there is to know about helping people. A lot of effort must be put in to it. Their Jewish religion teaches them of the Law and of work. But, the human soul will never be saved by the Law and hard work.

James: What to do?

Jesus: A new religion, really a return to a very old one, is the answer. The ancients were going along well when the Levites took over the temples.

James: What would you call it Jesus?

The Story of the Savior, Jesus of Nazareth

Jesus: THE WAY.

James: Can I help you?

Jesus: I will need lots of help, but it is all to be voluntary, never coerced. This is a Way into the future for all mankind.

James: I am ready - let's go!

The two planned and schemed over the next two weeks. Levi and others were brought in. Jesus would start his ministry in Jerusalem at the tender age of Thirty. His ministry was intended to "save" the world.

LATER – AT A NATURAL AMPHITHEATER

Anne, Mary, James, and Levi had selected a perfect spot outside of Jerusalem for Jesus - an address to a large group of men on their way to a Jewish festival for men in Jerusalem. The Pharisees were clever in the administration of rituals. Too many bring boredom and sameness. Too few and the people don't pay attention. If they are just right and interesting, they will have more impact on the minds that they attempt to control. Of course, it is all for the good of these poor people, who are working so hard that they don't have time to think about Jaweh. The priests do the thinking for them. If it works, you get unity.

The hillside was a natural amphitheater. Jesus would be elevated above the seated crowd on the level terrain below and in front of him. With some work, they had made a dirt and cement stage. They placed a small table at stage center. They removed all vegetation from the hillside. The acoustics were as good as could be expected. With help from Aaron, Isaac, and several others who had joined the assembly of the

The Way

Way, signs had been posted at strategic spots. These would lure any men they could to stop by on this Friday morning on the way to the festival in Jerusalem. "The Kingdom of God is at Hand," read the sign. "Come here, one Jesus of Nazareth explains to you what God hopes for your community. You do not need to be slaves to the Romans. God has a better idea." Some smirked and didn't pay any attention. Some, however, were curious enough to give it a try. They had nothing to lose and this might be a good spot to rest. The sign also read "Plenty of Water." James quick mind, coupled with his years at Qumran, could figure out how to get fresh water from here to there most of the time. James could smell an oasis in the desert. Some have saving talents they never knew they had until they test themselves.

They must have ushered in a few thousand men; men with sons, cousins, uncles, fathers, grandfathers and great grandfathers. The ushers got them all to settle down at ten o'clock a.m. They all worked the crowd with carts full of water jugs; most men had their own cup in their satchel. Some had brought food, some had not. There was the murmur of lots of men talking. Some stood while others were seated. Life was hard. Anything that God could do for them would be welcome news. Who was this assembly of the Way? They addressed God in different symbols than they do at the Temple in Jerusalem. Was it the same Jaweh? These people passing out water looked Jewish. They dressed like Jews. Was this another John the Baptist castigating the ones in authority but with no plan? The Baptist made them feel good for a little while, but then it was the same old thing. The Pharisee was in charge of religion, the Romans ran the state. These were the working masses. They were the flock that the Roman state and the Pharisaic religion fed off of. The Roman state had made a "strange bedfellows" alliance with the Pharisees in the governance of Judea. The governor, King Herod, a Jew, was a puppet. He wasn't a real king either. He snuggled up to the Romans and was in

The Story of the Savior, Jesus of Nazareth

with the wealthy. There were very few wealthy, but they controlled the money. They paid heavily to the Romans for protection. They wined and dined with the Romans, but Herod did not mingle with commoners. It was beneath his dignity. He depended on them for work, of course, but they were controlled by underlings far removed from him. It was a tryst. The High Priest, the Roman Prefect and the Jewish by birth (but not religion) Governor/King. The odd man out was the mass of people - Jews, Arabs, and Northern Africans, who did the dirty work. Their minds were controlled by religion. Their souls desperately sought a better way. Most souls ended their lives in despair. Perhaps this Jesus had something fresh. Doubtful. But most didn't have much to lose by at least listening.

James got up on the stage and, with palms pointing down to hush the crowd, said in a firm voice:

James: This morning I have the honor of introducing to you my friend Jesus - Jesus of Nazareth. Not far from here, next to the Roman enclave, is the small village of Nazareth. When he was a boy, he came to the festivals of Jerusalem and studied the Law, Prophets, and Writings - just as you. (There was murmuring. One man said to another, "Can anything good come out of Nazareth?" James put his palms down again, motioning the crowd to be quiet. Then he spoke again.) His mother and brothers still live there. His father was a mason who built structures for the Romans. Jesus apprenticed for his father. The Romans abused his father. His father never complained about working in the hot sun all day. The Romans respected the holy day, Saturday, but that was all. The Romans luxuriated in bathhouses while the common people worked. The Roman children were spoiled rotten. They thought that they were better than everybody else was. Their fathers were gone all the time. The mothers and servants raised the children in luxury. All this was supported by Caesar's army and police forces. You work and produce, they reap the benefits. Meanwhile the Pharisees convince you that you are no good sinners and need to sacrifice animals for atonement. You line up at the Temple for blocks with your sacrifices. You learned it from the Mosaic Law. It is deeply imbedded in your minds. Your lives are not your own. You are living someone else's life. The smoke goes up from the Temples' chimney all day and all night long. Rome says you are free men and that you are lucky you are not slaves, but I ask you to think about it. Many of you go out after working and get drunk so that you will not have to think about how miserable your lives are. You never see your families. Then you go back to work the next day still drunk to start the whole thing all over. Jesus will tell you this is not God's will for you.

A shout goes up from the crowd: "Then why doesn't Jaweh make it better for us? Why?" The crowd is really murmuring now. James has struck a sore spot, a nerve that makes one feel pain. "But what can we do about it? No one knows. We know of nowhere to hide."

Another says: "The Romans punish us if we don't do what they say."

James (with palms down quieting the crowd, speaks again): Jesus left Nazareth at fifteen years of age to go on a journey of discovery. Somebody had to do it. He spent many years far to the east. Twice as far as from here to the Caucasian Mountains, which many of you are told, is the end of the world. On the other side of the mountains the people are of a different skin color. Jesus will tell you how they are nevertheless the same as us. Jesus says that God loves differences, but he wants his world to be harmonious and for us to live in peace and love.

Chuckles go up from the crowd. "Tell the Romans about 'harmonious,'" shouts a grandfather type. "They want us to be harmonious slaves," shouts another. James, palms down, quiets the crowd.

The Story of the Savior, Jesus of Nazareth

James: Jesus learned from the masters of the Far East. He learned how some people of ancient times could live harmoniously. Jesus learned healing skills. He learned in the high mountains from the lamas. He in turn has much to teach you. He then spent many years in Rome as a mason's apprentice, where he learned architecture from Rome's best architect. He has built many buildings himself. He learned about the solid structure underlying the building. The entire structure might collapse if it has a weakness at its base. He will tell you that our society must be built in the same way. Its base must be secure, maintained. Without the constant maintenance of the base, eventually the structure will collapse. The structure is oblivious. We make the structure. God has given us the power to build. In him we move and have our being. Jesus has many things to say that may enlighten your minds. Listen to him. He has paid the price. He seeks nothing from you. He does not want to control you. If he can make your lives better, he figures that his life will be better too. May I introduce Jesus of Nazareth.

Jesus exuberantly hops up on the stage and hugs James. Mary, Anne, and the boys answer questions while many other helpers work the crowd with water carts. They had arranged for places with troughs that had some privacy. They didn't want the men complaining. Cleaning the place up after every one had left was the biggest chore. Levi had a group of young men working for him who would patrol the crowd, in case squabbles broke out. Men will argue about anything, given enough time. Things were tense in Palestine. They didn't want the tenseness erupting into something greater here.

Jesus: Good morning! (There was very little acknowledgement; after all they had never heard of him before.) Has anyone ever heard the name Melchizedek? (Murmurs, quizzical looks) Apparently you haven't. He is mentioned only

The Way

briefly in the Law, but let me tell you of the Savior Melchizedek!

That got the crowd going - "The Savior Melchizedek," what is this man talking about? Does he know what he is talking about?

Jesus (again): Melchizedek came before Abram. Abram paid tithes and alms to Melchizedek. Melchizedek was the King of Peace. Melchizedek founded Salem, which means "City of Peace." You now travel to that city for a festival. You call it Jerusalem.

(Murmurs: "this I didn't know," "how does he know this?" "The priests never told me of this.")

Jesus then said to them: Do not be in bondage to the past. You must be reborn. Your rulers even censor what is read to you by the priests. If you believe them, you are at their mercy. It was not Abram who abandoned Ishmael, it was later, when he was known as Abraham. Abram took Ishmael, his firstborn, into his tent and cared for him as he was taught by Melchizedek, even though Ishmael was born to Hagar. Sarai later bore him Isaac. We will never know the true story because it was taken from us. Our Patriarchs are not perfect, but they do not abandon their young. They do not kill women and children. Don't you understand? We are of a new covenant that listens to the past, but is not a slave to it.

Abram was a Hebrew - Hebrew means "wanderer." He probably was shoved out of his former home. He was a castaway. Melchizedek took him in and shared his home in Salem, the City of Peace. It is now Jerusalem. Oh, Jerusalem! If I could only take you under my wing and teach you. I am called a Jew. That comes from the name Judah. Judah was the fourth son of Jacob. Jacob was the last of the Hebrew Patriarchs.

The Story of the Savior, Jesus of Nazareth

Judah was the name given to a portion of southern Palestine, millennia in the past. The ancient writings have been molded by later writers to suit their present-day whims. When we do not know. You must know where things come from, or someone will take advantage of you. The ancient writings convey to us that man is both bad and good. Within him lies the divine. Within him lies the darkness. The Way wanders from its homeland to the light. It then brings back the lamp of light to the homeland. In the home we do not cover the light. We do not put it under a basket. No, we put in on a lamp stand so that all may see. The Philistines and the Hebrews shared their homeland. The Philistines were sea people. They would come and go. Come and go.

I tell you this so earnestly; it is everyone's world. Not just the few. The Kingdom of God beckons us. It is there ahead in the light. It is our responsibility to give the best of ourselves to the future, not the worst.

Jesus (goes on): Melchizedek founded a school at Salem. He founded a library at Salem. He founded a peaceful society of Canaanites. Melchizedek was born to the North, perhaps in Gaul. He was a mason by trade, a builder of secure structures. A very smart man. He was well trained in laws and healing. The ancient warlords way before the Greeks or the Romans had forced the Man of Peace to work for them, building cities to the north, even further north than Rome. He was appropriated by the men who used the sword. He revolted and led a group out into the wilderness of the east. The strong ones made it through or around the mountains and wilderness to the east of the Caucasians and finally through or around the greatest mountains in the world. I have seen them, I have drunk from their rivers of life, swam in the pools at the base of the Great Mountains where the remnants of Melchizedek's eastern society remain. They lived on the perimeters of the great Chinese deserts. Those expert in the use of horses and double-hump cam-

The Way

els could have a good life there. They were away from the most populated areas, where warlords fought for supremacy. Even China was changing into a dynastic culture. But that was near Peking and the great unsurpassable ocean. There, the masses of Chinese lived and became workers, just like you, for those who ruled by the sword. Melchizedek was an adventurer. He seemed so unlike everyone else. They thought of him as being on another level of existence. Little did they know that he paid the price of learning. He learned all the time. He never stopped. He was curious and had to try things out to see if they truly worked. He said that it was very important to give your best to society. That way we all benefit. He did not appreciate the indolent. He would get mad. "Get up off your ass you sluggard - do something to contribute."

By the same token, he was no slave driver and didn't believe in slavery. He thought that the biggest sin of all was to try to control another human being, either against his will with the use of physical violence or by the stealth of priestly mind control. He sought to enlighten the people, to teach the people. Their obligation in turn was to teach others. Simple things he said - how to tie a knot, how to sharpen the knife, how to stalk animals for food, to make clothes, to fish, to bake breads, to build boats. There is so much to learn, that no one need be idle except for necessary rest. He loved fun and playing. He loved laughing and singing. Make time for spiritual practices, like praying, fasting, and meditation. These spiritual practices will refresh your mind. He taught the Chinese that they were different, but really no different than the peoples of the West. That is except for the "coercers."

You see coercers of their fellow humans are the bane of the world. Melchizedek said that we should honor differences. He said it would be a boring life it everyone was the same. Can't you see that God loves variety?

The strong must help the weak. The superior must teach the inferior. The inferior can become superior. Is not the

The Story of the Savior, Jesus of Nazareth

teacher superior to the student? What is the relationship between them? That is the question. The teacher must be willing to teach. The student must be willing to learn. With this type of relationship, you will have progress in society. Teaching, learning, bettering our lives together. We must meet and be together and ritualize our commonalties. We must dig out anger, jealousy, and hatred at their roots. Two male siblings, one year apart, can be bitter enemies - more than two males from different lands. Welcome the stranger. Seek out the fatherless and bring them into the fold. We take care of one another's children, said Melchizedek. A smooth society can do more than the small family, but we must spread the kinship of the family to greater society. A society of kinship can do miracles.

Man is born into violence. You see it in history. James and Levi have built a wonderful library at Qumran. Its purpose is to store as much written knowledge as possible. This knowledge comes from the lands between the great unsurpassable ocean to the east at the far end of China, and the great unsurpassable ocean to the west on the far side of Gaul. We have etchings on stone tablets, we have papyrus rolls, we have vellum pages, and we have scratchings on copper sheets. On them are recorded our history. How to make bread. How to make wine. How to make cures for diseases and bruises to our bodies. How to operate on our bodies if need be. (There were oohs! and ahhs! to that one). There are records of man's wars. Levi and I counted one day the number of wars that we have recorded at the library, and this doesn't even count minor skirmishes and sieges by ignorants on fortified compounds. The total was 1457 and that's just what we have record of. The past has been a record of violence. I say to you, this should be proof to you that "an eye for an eye and a tooth for a tooth" just does not work. It's simple. How do we stop this endless cycle? The Way answers these kinds of questions. Do you know that there are some people who want constant war? They make their livelihoods on it. It is what they do. If we stick together you will

The Way

find that the innocents outnumber the rulers of war. And have you noticed that it's always the innocents that are killed in war. The elite impress the innocent into service and train them to be killers of other innocents. The rulers never die in war. They sit in the shadows and command the young men to fight to the death. Let us urge the rulers to battle, while we the innocent enjoy life.

Violence is a detour around learning. Improving your mind is the hardest work of all. The bully uses violence to coerce others to work for him. He knows it works. The warlords are bullies. The Caesars are bullies, the priests who make you believe you are no good sinners are bullies. The priests of the Levite Tent are bullies. The reason that Moses did not enter the Promised Land is simple. He sold his soul to violence.

The crowd begins to stir. This is becoming offensive to some ears. Moses is revered. The giver of the Law from God.

Jesus (continues): There were others far before Moses who brought the Law down from Heaven. The Buddha brought down the Law from Heaven, to free men not to enslave them. Melchizedek's "laws" were meant to make society smooth and straight. Moses was a Levite. He negotiated slyly the trade whereby the Levites took over the priestly duties. They gave up their single tribal rights to become the priests of the Temple. I have read their "Rules of War." They make all the Tribes participate in War without going themselves. The Generals report to them. They make them believe that they are advised by God. Moses was not a peacemaker. He derived his power from a band of slaves he convinced to come with him out of Egypt. Moses was a bully. He moved into the North with force of arms. He then usurped the peaceful "Assembly of the Way" people living in Judea. He took their land and their religion. The patriarchs Abram, Isaac, and Jacob and their descendants lived peacefully amongst the peoples of Melchizedek. They

The Story of the Savior, Jesus of Nazareth

were taught to do so. Violence was not of their heritage. They abhorred violence. They were peacemakers. Peacemaking was a hard job. Learning to better the community was a hard job. Abram, Isaac, and Jacob sought to keep the foundation of society strong for peace. Identify the bullies early on. They have been bullied. Give them love and bring them in to the community, do not let the rich and powerful lord it over the masses. Melchizedek said, "Blessed are the Peacemakers for they shall be called Sons of God." Melchizedek started a church for the Assembly of the Way, and they met once per week on Saturday. He did not sacrifice humans. He allowed Abram and his tent to sacrifice animals. Moses and his priests allowed the sacrificing of humans. As I told you, Moses did not reach the Promised Land. The Melchizedek Hebrews were called God's "chosen," based upon their penchant for peacemaking and building the structure of society with a sound base. For this they were "chosen" by God. Moses usurped this too. The Levites taunted others with their "chosen-ness." The Levites were the only ones left, along with the tribe of Judah. The other ten or eleven tribes were lost. Perhaps they continued a Diaspora to other lands, to avoid the coercive methods of the Levites. We'll never know.

In the Levite's Rules of War, we find that the priests and their generals were sacrificing the innocent young men of the lost ten tribes as their fodder in war. The safest thing was to be a Levite or a general. They never went to battle. But they ordered the young ones to their deaths. So long as the masses went along with this craziness, they had war after war after war. They fought either amongst themselves or an outside enemy. Generals have wars because that's what they do. They are praised and applauded only in times of war. The Levite priests control the mind because that's what they do.

You do not have to be like them. You must be reborn to see God's Kingdom. Don't you see? Don't you see? As you think so shall you act?

The Way

Lots of murmurs crescendo now amongst the crowd. It sounds good. However, there's one big catch. The Romans don't play fair in this hierarchy game, and they are rewarded for so doing. The dumb and the innocent are sacrificed in war, not the elite cartel. At least not most of the time.

A voice from the crowd: Jesus, the Romans don't play the game that way. We are way down here. They are way up there.

Jesus: Most Romans, unbeknownst to you, are whipping boys to the Caesar and his cronies. I tell you that we have them outnumbered. The problem with society since Moses is that the top few dominate the masses. The top few have always been the problem. Melchizedek, the Savior, did not Lord it over the people. They respected him because he did not try to take everything and leave them with scraps. I have lived in Rome for the past few years. I have seen the rich. It is harder for a rich man to see the Kingdom of God than it is for a camel to go through the "eye of the needle" to enter the City.

Voice from the crowd: What is rich?

Jesus: Rich is when you make money more important than people. When you make things more important than the life of the Spirit. Those things are part of the stage upon which we act. They are like props in a Greek play.

Jesus had to be careful that he didn't talk too long. He could have gone on for hours. He knew that they would not just learn from words. He needed action.

Jesus: We have supplied you with plenty of water, but you must be hungry by now. It is time for the noonday meal. Do all of you have food?

The Story of the Savior, Jesus of Nazareth

There was lots of murmuring now. Some had brought food. Some had not. Some were so skinny it looked like they hadn't eaten for days. They knew they would get free food at the festival.

James approached Jesus and told him that maybe half of the men had brought food.

Jesus: (With palms down, and with James helping him settle down the crowd.) At the Assembly of the Way we share food. It symbolizes our interdependence. Is there anyone here who would share his food with another? (Getting men to share is hard. Getting them to fight is easy.)

Jesus (again): I say is there anyone here who would share his food? We will provide water.

A little boy of maybe eleven or twelve years of age hopped up on the stage with his satchel.

Jesus: Aha! Little one do you have food to share?

The Boy: Here is my salted fish and bread. You can have as much of it as you want. I know how to get more.

Jesus: See you men, this little boy offers us his food. I thank him.

With that Jesus held up a piece of bread. He broke it and gave a morsel to the boy. He gave a morsel to James. He popped a morsel into his own mouth and with outstretched arms thanked the Universe for this little boy.

A voice from the crowd: I have bread and cheese to share.

The Way

Another voice: I have figs and olives to share.

And so it went, a chain reaction. The crowd became one, and when it was over there was still plenty left.

Jesus (looking into the eyes of the little boy): Little one, what is your name?

The Boy: My name is Thomas.

Jesus: Are you here with your father?

Thomas: I have no father.

Jesus: Do you have a mother?

Thomas: No.

Jesus: Do you want to change the world?

Thomas: I don't know what you mean.

Jesus: You said you knew how to get more food.

Thomas: I've had to learn. I can catch fish. I know how to preserve them by smoking them or salting them. I know how to make bread. I've had to learn.

Jesus: I already have two sons, Aaron and Isaac. I'd like you to meet them, they are here today with their mother Mary. You could be my third son if you like.

Thomas: (His face was radiant) You don't mean it?

The Story of the Savior, Jesus of Nazareth

Jesus: I wouldn't have said it if I didn't mean it.

Thomas: Can I meet them?

Jesus: Come with me.

Mary, Aaron, and Isaac fell immediately in love with this young man and they took him in. The crowd began disbursing to continue their trips, but not before they were briefed on the next meetings of the Assembly of the Way. Over the next three years, Jesus and his entourage traveled throughout Judea and Palestine. Many joined the Way and spread the word. Soon Jesus had enormous crowds on hand waiting for his next sermon. His sermons were ingenious. They were meant to assemble a group of spirited people who would find a better way than the Roman/Jewish priestly cartel had to offer.

Chapter Eighteen
Prince of the Herods

At an amphitheater in southern Palestine, James had noticed for the fourth straight time an entourage riding double-hump camels and the most beautiful Arabian horses he had seen in some time. What could these wealthy people be doing here? Just then, a huge African-looking man approached him. He was immaculately dressed and wore a turban. A sheath hung from his waist belt. It enclosed what must have been the biggest sword James had ever seen. The handle was highly polished teak wood. Jewels were imbedded in the handle. You wouldn't want to get in a fight with this fellow. He drew nearer and then stopped a few feet in front of James. Then he gracefully bowed. James was relieved. The man spoke Aramaic.

Jeremus: My name is Jeremus and I am here with a few other security guards from the House of Herod.

James (nervously): Have we done something wrong?

Jeremus: No! The House of Herod does not know that we are here. We protect one of the family princes. We have been at some of your gatherings and have always sat near the rear. The prince does not wish to be seen. He is infatuated with your Jesus of Nazareth. The young man would be most grateful if Jesus would meet with him in private. We will pay you well. Could you arrange this?

James: There are no private places around here. People will be milling around here for quite some time.

The Story of the Savior, Jesus of Nazareth

Jeremus: We will put up tents for the comfort of Jesus and the prince. We have water and dried fruits and fish. We will fan them as they talk. You may bring your own people to stand guard outside the tent

James: Stay here. I will go find Jesus and ask him.

James shuffles back to the front of the amphitheater. He gathers together the inner group—Anne, Mary, Levi, Aaron, Isaac, Thomas, and their newest convert Nicodemus, a Pharisee. Convert meant that you felt a kindred spirit with the Way. It was like a larger family of Man. It was a communion of all peoples of the known world that stretched from the unsurpassable ocean to the west, to the unsurpassable ocean to the Far East. Jesus felt that if they shared some common values, they would be less likely to skirmish with one another. It was a "safe harbor."

No one would be armed with a weapon while in the environ of the Way. The Way was supported by anonymous gifts. No one was to judge another by how much money was given. Jesus was not against the use of money. It certainly made trading and maintaining the structure of society a lot easier. What he was against was the use of the money supply as a "control mechanism" by the most aggressive males. It was the number two method of control, after violence. Number three, thought Jesus, was religion. The warlords of the past had in many cases learned to cozy up to the leaders of a conquered people's religion. Depending upon the conqueror's success, the very religion itself would begin changing. Special wording was inserted here and there. Most people couldn't read or write anyway. They were the pawns in this game of chess.

The prophets of old knew all about this. The prophets had their ways of countering the recurring dominator's schemes. In the end the prophets were persecuted by the dominators. Very seldom would a prophet persecute a dominator.

Prince of the Herods

An assassination once in a very great while. The dominators were usually too well protected to get anywhere near them. Nevertheless, the dominators were all paranoid and learned to nip the bud early, before the prophet could incite the pawns. Isaiah was forced to look for someone of superhuman qualities to liberate the pawns. Jesus sought to raise them to a level above pawnhood. Jesus sought to put an end to the recurring cycle. Life was for everyone. A good life. It wasn't for just the few. After James had cornered everyone, he shouted to Jesus.

James: Jesus, come talk to us for a moment.

They all sat in a circle on the ground. James explained to the group what this little meeting was about. Of course, many thought this to be some sort of set-up. After all, the famous John the Baptist had been beheaded at the House of Herod. Herod was not well liked by the populace.

Jesus: I know all about the House of Herod. In Rome, at one of the libraries, Mary would sit with me while I studied our history. You don't know how well to trust these writers because you do not know their purpose. I read enough to get a good idea of where the Herods got their bad reputation.

Levi: I suppose Isaac and Aaron were studying hard, too?

Mary: They were busy studying Roman girls. Tell them what you learned Isaac.

Isaac: We learned that they like Jewish boys, right Aaron?

Aaron: There are a few of them that would like to come to Jerusalem. Can we invite them?

The Story of the Savior, Jesus of Nazareth

Everyone was laughing now. Isaac and Aaron were just as nervy now as when they were kids. Jesus knew how to channel their aggressiveness in the right direction and never let them get too "full of themselves."

Anne: Aren't you worried this might be some kind of a set-up?

Jesus: What do you think James? I'm very curious about this person. I'd like to meet him. Just think, a royal Prince forsaking the good life and joining up with us.

James: What do you mean, good life? He has no idea what a good life is. That's why he's asking to meet with you.

Jesus: I was joking, James.

James: It doesn't seem like a set-up to me.

Nicodemus: I'm curious about what Jesus found out about the royal Herods.

Jesus: "Royal" my ass. They are a bunch of snakes. The grandfather was of Northern African blood. He was interested only in money and power. People were merely a means to his ends. He went a step further than the mere trading of goods. He wanted control of everything. Herod the Great was in with the copper miners. They needed cheap labor and he was in competition with others of his same ilk. They fought for supremacy over who would control the mines. He was defeated in a war with others that would control the wealth of the people.
    Herod did not like losing and came up with a scheme to enrich himself and the Levite rulers of Jerusalem, the Pharisees. He went to Rome to make liaison with the rich and powerful.

Prince of the Herods

Herod, being skilled in trading, helped the Romans with some problems they were having on the Silk Roads. After ingratiating himself, he convinced them that he could be influential in Palestine with procurement of natural resources from that area, such as copper. He told them he was a Jew and influential in the religion that controlled the minds of the people in the region. One Senator asked him which tribe he was from, and he told him the "House of Herod."

The Romans, being as greedy as the Herods, agreed to use their army to make Herod "King of the Jews." They made Palestine a Protectorate of the Empire. Herod's head was anointed with oil by the Pharisees in a ceremony ritualizing him as the "King of the Jews." As long as Herod took care of the Pharisees in Jerusalem and the Romans in Rome, with taxes and natural resources, everything was just fine and the Roman soldiers insured "stability." Stability was for the upper crust. The people were the pawns. Herod built a colossal compound near the Dead Sea. He was so rich that he went wherever he wanted, whenever he wanted. He ruled by violence. He had several wives and lots of little princes. He fathered children that he didn't know he fathered. Everyone feared him except the Pharisees and the Romans. As long as he delivered the goods, he was the good king.

The grandfather died about when I was born. The House of Herod continued with one of the princes as ruler when the Romans split up the protectorate between Archelaus and Antipas. The Jews, after years of cruelty by Herod I, had petitioned to become a protectorate of Syria, but were denied. Herod Archelaus proved to be inept and was put out to pasture in France. Antipas then took over the entire region and is who we have the pleasure of dealing with today.

They all broke out in laughter.

The Story of the Savior, Jesus of Nazareth

James: That's where Jeremus said they came from, a compound near the Dead Sea, the House of Herod.

Jesus: Antipas is the one who had the "Baptist" beheaded.

Nicodemus: Why did he do this, Jesus?

Jesus: You a Pharisee and you don't know?

Nicodemus: The High Priest is very secretive.

Jesus: The Baptist was a revolutionary.

Levi: How so?

Jesus: The Pharisees were losing customers to the Baptist. In order to transfer or absolve sin at the Temple, the people had to pay. Both with animals for sacrifice and tithes. John absolved them with water. It was free. Neither did John demand tithes. They gave to him of their free will. This was big trouble. The Pharisees wanted something done about this. The Baptist was also trying to free them of their ultimate bondage, the Romans.

Herod Antipas was as much a schemer as his father. He had married his brother's wife, Herodias. The Baptist, in one of his tirades against the authority of Rome and its henchmen, referred to Herodias as an adulteress and her relationship with Herod as sinful adultery. Unfortunately for John, it was the straw that broke the camel's back and cost him his head. At a lavish party, where Herod was drunk on whatever substance he was happening to be using and Herodias dancing enticingly before him, he granted her a wish for pleasing him. I suppose this included leaving her former husband. As you all know by

Prince of the Herods

now, she asked for John's head on a platter. Business got better at the Temple in Jerusalem soon thereafter.

James: What a bunch of snakes! If you meet with this prince, we will take precautions. We will send a hundred men ahead to jump on them if they kidnap you and try to take you to the evil compound.

Jesus: Good. Now go and inform them that I will meet with this prince.

After James and the rest of the group made arrangements so that they would feel comfortable with the situation, Jesus went to the tent of the House of Herod. There sat an attractive young man, perhaps around 20 years of age, sitting on comfortable pillows which were ornately designed. His clothing appeared to be made from silk and linen. He was being fanned by two huge men of Northern African descent. Jesus was met by Jeremus, who wore a big, beautiful smile. He bowed to Jesus and asked Jesus if he would touch him. Jesus embraced this huge man in his arms as tears of joy dripped from Jeremus' eyes. The young man approached Jesus and bowed. When he straightened up, he introduced himself as Prince Agrippa and Jesus stepped forward and embraced him too.

They sat on the pillows for a long while trading stories. One story Jesus told him was about when he worked for Ashkenazy raising and training horses. He told Agrippa about how Ashkenazy had learned from those before him about breeding horses for the job that you want them to do. Some types of animals will interbreed to produce something different. Some types of animals will not interbreed at all. Some will produce offspring that are different, but are sterile. They themselves do not reproduce. He told him that three of Ashkenazy's five wives were Chinese, but that Ashkenazy was from the

The Story of the Savior, Jesus of Nazareth

north and did not look much different than the two conversationalists themselves. The children from these marriages produced offspring that looked half-Aramaic and half-Chinese. Jesus felt that all humans along the Great Way were basically the same, and that building communion between all of them was for the good of everyone.

Prince Agrippa told Jesus that he was becoming increasingly dissatisfied with life inside the House of Herod. Everyone seemed so selfish and had to get their way. They learned it from the "King" himself, whom Agrippa thought of as arrogant and treacherous. How to get a real life was Agrippa's paramount question of Jesus. Jesus was more than happy to give him suggestions.

Jesus: Have you ever heard of a man named Gautama Siddhartha?

Prince: No.

Jesus: He was a young man, just like you, born into wealth in India.

Prince: To the east on the "Silk Road"?

Jesus: Yes, and he had the same problem. The religion, once pure, now allowed the few to rule over the many. It was said to be the natural way. The few should get most of everything and the many would get what was left over. He didn't think it was right. He left the wife that had been chosen for him and his children. They weren't his by free will anyway. He left the life of riches and security, with nothing in his pocket, to go on a "journey of discovery." Discovery of himself and the world with which he interacted. He looked for the smartest minds in the world. Already there were libraries in China. He had heard of the masters of the Tao Te Ching in China. That is

Prince of the Herods

where he went. They sent him to the Highest Mountain to seek the Tao. There he meditated on all he had learned. He congealed everything with his highest consciousness. He became what they called the Buddha. Buddha means understand or awaken. The Buddha then went down from the mountain to teach.

Prince: What does all this mean to me?

Jesus: Buddha taught that you could attain Buddhahood too. There is a price, a big price. For a time you must leave on this pilgrimage. You will know when it's time to come back. We can help you with a curriculum. It is you that must have the desire. You could spend time with us to learn some basics. Then we would help you set up a journey.

Prince: How long will it take?

Jesus: It took me all of fifteen years and it may take longer or it may be shorter. In truth I learn every day. You let us know. It must come from your free will, or you will not get the full effect. The more you want it, the more it will be given to you.

Prince: I must mull this over in my mind. This is all new to me.

They both arise and Jesus embraces him one more time. Jeremus and his helpers fold up the tents, as the Prince sits in the shade thinking and munching on dried figs. Jesus returns to his group to plan their next event. He never saw the prince again.

The Story of the Savior, Jesus of Nazareth

ONE MONTH LATER

Mary: Welcome to our fifth meeting here in Jerusalem, the City of Peace. Today, hundreds of new faces are here to hear a message of hope from Jesus of Nazareth. He does not seek to destroy the Law and the Prophets. No, no - but they must be fulfilled. Isaiah was bold enough to define God for us. That is only part of God. We can never know the fullness of God, but we can know something. He is a God of justice, of mercy, and of love for one's neighbor. We at the Way are bold enough to speak for him. I introduce to you Jesus of Nazareth, who will tell you about the Way.

Jesus: New wine cannot be kept in an old wineskin. The old wineskin has become taught. There is no resilience left in it. It is too rigid, too lifeless. The Way is old, and yet it is new, because it changes. We are not set in our ways. The Law was set by people living many generations before us. We do not force those old ideas on today's minds. We do not say an eye for an eye and a tooth for a tooth. That is a recipe for disaster. The circle of violence never stops. Man is born violent. Violence begets violence. It never stops. You must be born again into the Kingdom of God. The Kingdom is within you. You can ask yourself, "Shall I continue the cycle of violence?" No! Show your enemy kindness when he seeks to lure you into a fight. Give the bully the love that he so desperately seeks. You complain about the Romans, treat them with respect and love. That does not mean that you have to give in to them. To take up the sword against the Romans would be foolish. That is their game. They rule by fear. You can choose not to give in to fear.

Mary and Jesus had impressed many with their healing skills, learned mostly in China, but also at Qumran. Jesus' idea was to build a library in Jerusalem with the most up to date information available. It would be sponsored by the Way. He wanted to have places for boys like Thomas, Aaron, and Isaac, who had no families. That was one of Jesus' ideas for the maintenance of the foundation of society.

Jesus (again): We have problems not only with the Romans but from a religion that seeks to dominate our minds. Listen to me please. Moses himself was an abandoned male baby. He became a bully because of it. We must seek to build society the good way. Bullies take freedoms from you; they are doing to you what was done to them. Moses was hung up on sex but not on violence. Sex is for life. Violence is for death. Moses had it backwards, and he was not allowed to reach the Promised Land. Don't you see? We can break free of the ones who would control us rather than help us. We cannot do it by violence. Otherwise we are them. We must learn to live together, to love one another despite our differences. Melchizedek lived in peace with the Chinese people. He lived in peace here in Judea with the Canaanites. He brought Abram into his bosom. Abram and Abram's heirs. Those are your Jewish ancestors. They were chosen by God because they were peaceful and worked together for better lives without violence. Peace must be taught. It is a constant job of maintenance of society. If society is left to the vile nature of man it will be destroyed. Listen to me, please. I speak the truth. The Way is the way of truth. It changes as we change. Its work is constant. The Way says that you can change the world. Armies and swords are not the Way.

Chapter Nineteen
The Voice of the Sage

Jesus and his entourage from the Way had become popular beyond their wildest expectations. Huge throngs would gather wherever they went. They performed amazing healings all over Palestine. They were a traveling road show. Some things that Mary and Jesus learned in China were applied to the Arabs and the Jews in Palestine. Not everything worked. Anne and James tried to keep track of what worked and what didn't. With their tiring schedule it was hard. Maybe in the future, the libraries could be used to store this data so one could look at the "big picture." Now it was all they could do to satisfy the throngs that followed them. With practice comes confidence, and the Way now dared not only to speak for God, but to speak in the very midst of the Pharisees domain. Most Jews didn't think for themselves on these matters. The High Priest was the interpreter of the ancient scriptures. He interpreted the scriptures for the masses. The people had so many questions that couldn't be answered by interpretation of the Law, that the High Priest and his appointees created a whole new body of writings. These were meant to add to the scriptures and apply them to the world of Jerusalem as it was now, not just in Moses time. Just exactly what was work? If it was a sin to work on Shabbat, would they be sinning if they helped their Arab neighbor put out a fire in his house? The word "sin" was the 20th letter of the Hebrew alphabet. In the Bible, the word "sin" is most succinctly defined as "lawlessness" - breaking the Mosaic Law.

Moses then appointed the Levites to be the priests and define sin for the other tribes. Moses knew how to handle people who didn't agree with him or his priests. An elaborate set of

The Voice of the Sage

rituals was set up, including the sacrificing of animals for all kinds of things, not just sins. They were called "burnt offerings," because they burned the animals and the smoke rose symbolically, as it were, to the domain of Jaweh that was above somewhere.

Then too, the masses were required to tithe to the Levites to support them as they worked for the "tabernacle." The Tabernacle was in the wilderness, in a high place called Gideon. Centuries later, a young man by the name of David, who traced his lineage from the tribe of Judah became the King of Israel. He said that a "House" for the Lord must be built in Jerusalem, to hold the "Ark of the Covenant." It should no longer be housed in the wilderness. David hired foreigners who were knowledgeable in building buildings. They were called "masons." David, being both a compassionate man but also a man of war, was not allowed to complete the process. He felt it was because God thought that David had too much blood on his hands. One of David's sons, Solomon, would inherit the job. David suggested it would be a time of rest for Israel, a time of prosperity. Now things get confusing between "tribes" and "houses." Were there 12 tribes or 13 tribes? At any rate, Solomon inherits the concept of "Houses." This is all "chronicled" in I and II Chronicles.

King Solomon had inherited a nice deal. You might say he reaped what he had not sown. It was Moses who made the Levites the priests. It was his father David who made the tribe of Judah the rulers. What about the other 10 tribes? Well let's say it this way, "someone has to do the work." A sweet little hierarchical system. When one looks at the structure of the inorganic Universe, one could use the metaphor of "hierarchy" to explain gravitational selection. One could also detect "pattern integrities." If the inorganic world is so structured, is it not unlikely that one might see the same tendencies in the organic world that arose spontaneously from the inorganic.

The Story of the Savior, Jesus of Nazareth

King Solomon talked to God twice. Both times in the middle of the night. It probably came in a dream. So Solomon moved from Gideon to Jerusalem (some call it the City of David), and built the Temple with the plans already put in place by his father. One hundred and eighty three thousand foreigners led by "master craftsmen" and alien, Hiram, built the Temple in honor of Solomon's father. So the 10 tribes worked in their appointed jobs, while "foreigners" built the Temple. According to King Solomon, God was giving him a big bundle. At this point in history, might we guess that Solomon would recognize his good fortune and share much of his wealth with the 10 worker tribes? Are we supposed to overcome human nature or submit to human nature? Maybe it doesn't have to be either/or. Maybe sometimes we do and sometimes we don't. The most important thing to know perhaps is "just what is human nature, anyway?" My guess is that Solomon will get his hands on as much as he can, justify it, and worry about the consequences later. Meanwhile, you could say that there was order in society. This order will only last so long. The Hebrew Bible attests to this. Out of Solomon's disproportionate prosperity came trouble.

Wars ensued leading to the destruction of the Temple. The King of the Chaldeans took all the treasure, killed the men and women (except virgins), and returned with the booty to Babylon. Oh yes, not all were killed - some were taken as slaves to work for their new masters. After all this time, after the slaves had been led out of Egypt, now they were back in captivity. History sometimes repeats itself.

Cyrus, King of Persia, reversed the bad fortunes of the Jews and released them and the treasures stolen (taken in war) by the Chaldeans. Now, a second Temple was built in Jerusalem. This Temple was to last until the mighty Roman Army burned it to the ground in 70 AD, in reprisal for Jewish zealots not abiding by Roman rules. Wars from within, wars from without. Your laws, my laws. Kings, then revolutionaries.

The Voice of the Sage

Then, the revolutionaries become kings who are then dispatched by external wars of aggression or civil wars. Wars of civilians against their own government. Who could find unity in this quagmire of history?

We now pick up in a sermon delivered a month later, where Jesus had left off:

>Jesus of Nazareth (now preaching in the second Temple): The Way does not look for unity. Unity doesn't work. Can't you look at history and see the endless chain of man's wars with himself? The Way puts forth the idea of "community." We should rejoice and be thankful for our differences. We would have a boring, stagnant world if everyone looked the same, thought the same, and acted the same. Look at the variety present in nature. Are we not part of nature? Yet, we have the ability to look at it and decide what's good and bad about it.
>
>Community means recognizing that we are delightfully different, yet we are delightfully the same. A good paradox. We also recognize that it's a bad paradox. We naturally fight with one another about our differences. I have something to tell you. It doesn't have to be this way. When we commune, we act as peacemakers between the differing parts of the whole. We act as the Saviors that Melchizedek urged us to be. Melchizedek shared bread and wine with Abram. It was a symbolic communion of their brotherhood, even though they came from different tribes. Melchizedek, rather than turn Abram away, lived in community with him.
>
>When I was in China, I was given a copper scroll. Etched on it was language from Melchizedek himself. The etchings are in the library of the Way. One says "The field is ripe, but the laborers are few." Melchizedek was looking for saviors of the world. The Prophet Isaiah in the Jewish Scriptures was looking for a savior. A savior cannot do it alone; the field of harvest is too big. We need saviors in the world today to answer the call of Isaiah. Saviors do not come to heal the

The Story of the Savior, Jesus of Nazareth

healthy. They come to heal the sick. Saviors make the community better by tending to its very base - the poor, the weak, the innocent. They bring them up the ladder.

A voice rings out from the back of the Temple. "The Romans don't want Saviors, they want slaves." Many voices echo this sentiment as the crowd murmurs. Jesus, James, Levi, and Aaron all try to hush the crowd.

Jesus (again after the crowd quieted): The Romans are a good example of what we must not be like. We must listen to the wisdom of the past. We must listen to the voice of the Prophet. We must listen to the voice of the "Sage." Then we must answer Isaiah's call for the "Son of Man." Isaiah was a Prophet and a Sage. The new man must be created. He is the antithesis of the leaders of the world today. The Son of Man first understands his violent nature. He then overcomes it and becomes a productive member of society. He teaches the children after he has learned himself. The Son of Man never stops learning. He is continuously recreating himself for the service of mankind, not the dominance of mankind. Melchizedek etched on the cooper scroll, "I came to seek and to save that which is lost." He said, "Come learn from me. I will share my hard-earned knowledge with you."

He said, "I am like a well. You can keep drawing from me and not thirst." The Son of Man walks, talks, and lives with the people. He does not live in a palace with servants to indulge his every whim. The Son of Man gives service to the rest of mankind to make lives better. He does not use the innocent and prey upon them. He lifts them up to new horizons. He gives them Hope. He is God's servant. In this he fulfils himself and becomes brand new. He has lost his old self to gain his new self.

The Voice of the Sage

The crowd is really getting inspired by Jesus' confidence. The Pharisees do not talk this way. They do not think this way. Jesus challenges them to become more than they are. He resonates with most. The spies in the Temple do not even listen to his words. The words bounce off deaf ears.

Jesus now walks amongst the seated crowd and talks as he goes.

Jesus: My friend James and I sit beneath the stars or beside a crackling fire and ask why some people are born into misery while others are born into luxury. Some who are born into misery escape its grip and are intensely motivated to join the elite. Many do not remember where they came from. Some who are born into luxury do not appreciate what they have. For every one that lives in luxury there are many who live in misery. The Son of Man creates the Kingdom of God by helping the Father. The keys to the Kingdom are in his hands. If we do not answer Isaiah's call, we are doomed to the recurring cycle of violence. Violence begets violence. You have heard it said, "An eye for an eye and a tooth for a tooth." You may feel vindicated by returning vengeance on the perpetrator. But it doesn't solve the problem. Can you not see over the millennia that "an eye for an eye and a tooth for a tooth" just does not work? You must discover the root of the problem that causes the cycle of violence and figure out what you can do about it. Injustice amongst peoples must be ferreted out and destroyed. Injustice is a big cause of violence. "Blessed be the Peacemakers," said Melchizedek, "for they shall be called 'Sons of God.'" Peacemaking is a full time job. It makes sense for society to maintain its foundation, because that it is where revolutions come from. Revolutionaries don't come from the elite. The elite bring wars of conquest. They have the innocents fight their battles for them. If we do not create this "Son of Man," the cycle will continue for millennia to come until the earth is de-

The Story of the Savior, Jesus of Nazareth

stroyed. The weapons of destruction will be so fine-tuned that you will be able to kill your fellow man without even watching him die.

One teenager asks Jesus what God's "will" is.

Jesus: Listen everyone (Jesus wants attention on this one.) Young man, get up and introduce yourself.

Young Man: My name is Jeremiah and I want you to tell us what God's will is for me.

Jesus embraces the young man and, smiling, asks him to sit again.

Jesus: You should all be asking yourself this question all the time. If you seek an answer you will find it. But I won't dodge the question. God asks you to seek Salvation. Saved from what I ask you? Saved from what you are! You must seek a higher level for yourself.
This process never stops but it has levels, just as ice turns to water, so you can become a new creature. Then the water turns to steam as the fire chastens the water. Your Father in Heaven chastens those he loves.

Jesus always talked in comparative symbolism. Language is meant to convey states of the psyche: its moods, its feelings, and its desires. Sometimes those states can be described best in indirect methods. Jesus himself said that you cannot look directly at the Father, you only see Him indirectly. Therefore, you do not see all of Him. He also cautioned that we are prisoners of the language that we use. God is not male or female. We convey our perceptions through words. But words have edges where one slips silently into another. People communicate in many ways, said Jesus. He was taught that in the

The Voice of the Sage

Far East. Learn all that you can, but live by your feelings. Some had trouble understanding his metaphoric skills. He told them that as they practiced one day it would dawn on them. Perseverance has its rewards.

Jesus (continuing): Your salvation is revealed in this world. Your salvation is interconnected with those less fortunate than yourself. As you do unto them, you do unto the Father. Righteousness is a state of mind, but it is revealed in your actions. You are the liberator, not the oppressor. You heal the sick. You take in the abandoned children. Is not becoming "better" at least part of the idea of "Salvation"? Salvation never stops. What we must do is define what "better" means. You teach love to the male child from when he is young to when he is old. You visit the prisoners. You feed the hungry. You build the buildings to shelter the people. You kick the lazy in their backsides. You try to understand the plight of the inebriated and the prostitutes. You do not judge your fellow man. I could go on and on - that's why I teach every Saturday to all who will listen.

A voice from the crowd: Rabbi, is there life after death?

Jesus: You should ask, "Is there life after birth?" What is life anyway? Is it toiling for the Romans? Then getting drunk to forget about your troubles? I am here to give you life, and give it to you more abundantly. Let God worry about life after death.

Another voice: Rabbi, you never speak directly.

Jesus: When you look at a star, it is best seen when you look at it indirectly. The Kingdom of God can best be seen indirectly

The Story of the Savior, Jesus of Nazareth

A voice from the crowd: What about the Torah?

Jesus: I respect the Torah. We must have laws. The Romans have laws. The Buddha came down from Heaven with the Law. You are not saved by the Law. You are saved only by the way you think. Do not be judgmental. Only the Father can judge. But we must have earthly laws to prevent anarchy. On the bottom of society are the lawless. They are lawless on account of their ignorance. At the top of society are the lawless. They are lawless by the corruption of greed and power. Too much greed and too much power. They are not givers, they are takers. Society only benefits from their leftovers.

Another voice: What do we do to change?

Jesus: Learn and act. Learn and act. We at the Way are teachers. We teach reading to the children. We teach reading to the adults. We have had copiers make copies of not only the Jewish Writings, but also the writings of the Buddha and Lao-Tzu. You can read them at our locations around Palestine. We suggest that you join our cause. We are an antidote to the poison of the Roman mind. We spread love, not violence. We outnumber the elite. It is not just their world, it is everyone's world. But we must stand up to them with love, not violence. Listen to the words of Lao-Tzu.

Jesus quotes from memory. He pretends he is with Wa-Lu beside an oasis water pond, tossing pebbles and quoting the Masters:

"I have three treasurers that I cherish and hold dear
The first is love.
The second is moderation.
The third is humility.

The Voice of the Sage

With Love one is fearless.
With moderation one is abundant.
With humility one can fill the highest position.
Now if one is fearless but has no love,
    abundant but has no moderation,
    rises up but has no humility,
Surely he is doomed.

Love vanquishes all attackers.
It is impregnable in defense.
When Heaven wants to protect someone
    does it send an army?
No, it protects him with love."

One hears sighs and moans from the crowd. Jesus goes on.

Jesus: The Buddha would say that you are part of something greater. The greater is in process, as you are in process. You are not what you were yesterday. Today you are different than what you will be tomorrow. Our self is part of a greater Self. We ourselves aren't the Way, but we can affect our course and therefore its course. Some would say that the Buddha does not see the building of the Kingdom of God. Some say that Moses was Holy. The Buddha that I believe in sought to overcome the world, not be its whipping boy. The Buddha I know said, "enmities are never appeased by enmity, but they are appeased by non-enmity. This is the eternal law." The Moses I know said to his officers of his army, "now therefore, kill every male among the little ones, and kill every woman who has known a man intimately. But keep alive for yourselves all the young girls who have not known a man intimately." Moses performed great terror in the sight of all Israel.

The Story of the Savior, Jesus of Nazareth

Jesus knew that if he went on too long he would lose them. He chose to now turn over the stage to James. He asked to close with a prayer.

Jesus: My friend James is waving to me to stop talking, so that you won't get tired of me.

There were chuckles and laughs from the crowd.

Jesus: Could I ask you to bow your heads for a prayer?

Heads all went down.

Jesus: Father, we ask that we might first seek your Kingdom of Righteousness with the knowledge that our needs will be met, that we love our fellow man as we love ourselves. Amen.

James, Anne, and several others now occupy stage center. Levi and the boys (Isaac, Aaron, and Thomas) are at the exits to introduce themselves to possible converts. James explains that there will be a ceremony for taking in new members at their amphitheater. They didn't want to do it in the Temple. Jesus didn't know how much he was playing with fire. One day he had chased a bunch of moneychangers out of the Temple, not because they were moneychangers, but because they were greedy moneychangers. They took advantage of the elderly and the widows, who were not as knowledgeable as the worldly men. On the other hand, he was high profile and always drew crowds wherever he went. He was a deep well and the people thirsted. It's a shame that his body of knowledge was not allowed to reach fruition. Some saw him as a threat to their more pragmatic ways of dealing with "reality."

Chapter Twenty
The Powers That Be React

The message was said in many different ways. In as many different metaphors as Jesus and James could dream up. But there was a problem. A big problem. Spies from the Synagogue and spies from the Roman Prefect's office, whose job it was to know everything that's going on, reported to their higher-ups the "dangerous" ideas of the Way. The High Priest and the Prefect Pontius Pilate met to discuss the subject at the High Priest's inner chambers.

Pilate: You are losing your constituency to an itinerant religious nut. Some no good, like John the Baptist, who Herod had beheaded. No one took up the Baptist's mantle after that. Herod got great applause from Rome.

High Priest: This Jesus is a thorn in my side. Jews who have brought in their animals for sacrifice for years, we no longer see. Our revenues have been cut drastically. This can't go on.

Pilate: Tax collection has been the same story. They aren't paying up. Nor are they working in the copper mines as they were. This Jesus has told them that the mines aren't safe and that we don't pay enough to make the risk worthwhile. I have only so many prisoners of war to work with; I have only so many slaves. The people clamor for aqueducts and roads. I don't have anyone to work on them. I've had to send them back to the copper mines, because that's Rome's number one priority. They need copper for their armies. It's a good thing these igno-

The Story of the Savior, Jesus of Nazareth

rants don't know anything about bathhouses and stadiums, or they would be really edgy.

      High Priest: We need action now. But I don't know what to do.

      Pilate: I do. Listen to my plan.

      Pilate outlined a nefarious plan whereby the High Priest would drum up some charge against Jesus. The Jewish priests would hand Jesus over to Pilate. Pilate would take care of the rest. Pilate did not tell the priests the whole story. He had another plan to blame them for the sordid affair. He had learned from his superiors to always make the Romans appear to be the helpers, not the instigators. The Romans had always been good at scheming. They would start wars by sacrificing their own men in an effort to pin blame on a foe they wished to goad into war. They would send a mission of twenty men to meet with the Germans. In the dark of the night, Roman soldiers dressed as Germans would slaughter the mission members and leave them gruesomely scattered about, with German weapons protruding from their mouths or bellies. They would carve anti-Roman graffiti on their faces and chests. There was nothing sacred to the Roman war machine.

Chapter Twenty-One
The Teachings of the Way

It is one month later. Jesus is preaching today in Jerusalem about what the Way stands for. There were many spies in the huge crowd.

James: Anne, will you help me get some of these papyrus signs up?

Anne, James, and Levi, with much help, had made numerous posters explaining the whys and wherefores of the Way. One poster read:

THE **WAY** STANDS FOR:

1.) Peacemaking as a Way of life.
2.) The Brotherhood of all Peoples.
3.) Responsibility of the Individual.
4.) Teaching as a life long pursuit.
5.) Learning as a life long pursuit.
6.) Giving to the future.
7.) The superiors are obligated to help the inferior.
8.) Forgiving those who have trespassed against you.

Another read:

THE **WAY** TEACHES:

1.) Men and Women to be "artisans."
2.) Children to honor their parents.
3.) Parents to honor their children.

The Story of the Savior, Jesus of Nazareth

4.) Children without a parent or parents are to be taken in by others and to be loved.
5.) Children have a responsibility to learn.
6.) Everyone has the responsibility to contribute to society.
7.) Spiritual Practices, such as prayer, meditation, fasting, giving of yourself to the poor and needy, the sick, and the imprisoned, should be practiced. Over and over until they become natural.
8.) The Way is a "Spiritual Church."

Another read:

THE PATRIARCHS OF THE WAY ARE:

1.) Melchizedek
2.) Abram
3.) Isaac
4.) Jacob
5.) Joseph
6.) Lao-Tzu
7.) The Buddha

Another read:

THE WAY TEACHES:

1.) Healing the body.
2.) Healing the mind.
3.) Healing the soul.
4.) Doing unto others as you would have done unto you.
5.) Serving people, not lording it over them.

The Teachings of the Way

6.) Sharing knowledge.
7.) Anticipating problems in society.

    Anne introduced Jesus to the crowd. Jesus was primed and ready to go. He feels like he could talk and teach for hours. He knows he must be as succinct as he can be. The attention span of the audience is not long.

    Jesus: I merely bring to you a Way that never really dies - it has always been here. Our patriarchs are men of peace. They build society peacefully. Society must be maintained. When envy grows amongst men there is trouble. When some men display their greed in public, there will be trouble. The ancient Greeks called this Hubris. Hubris is the natural inclination of the Prince of the World. Lao-Tzu taught about the Prince. The Buddha left his home in India because of the Prince. He knew that the Prince of the World did not know the Way. The Prince orders the artisans around. He is not an artisan himself. He does not know art and artists and artistry.

    A voice came from the crowd.

    Voice: Jesus, do you believe in Jaweh?

    Jesus: Whose Jaweh?

    The crowd laughs and murmurs.

    Another voice: You are the rabbi, not us.

    Jesus: Read Isaiah. I believe in Isaiah's God. A God of justice. But also a God who has given us Free Will. Our most precious gift. Can't you see that God loves diversity in all things? We must be the light of the world. We must illuminate justice and live it out. With variety comes difference. With difference, the strong and the weak.

A voice: If you ask me, God is cruel.

Jesus: Our work is to make human lives better. Everyone's life better. We find our lives have meaning when we help solve one another's problems. Life is for living. Helping your fellow man brings a feeling of happiness and joy. Do not promote war. Promote peace. Do not make your neighbor envious of you. Melchizedek believed in saving the world, not being the Prince of the World. Melchizedek said that a peacemaker is God's Son.

A voice: You are a Jew, why do we need this Way? We have the Law.

Jesus: You cannot be saved by the Law. The religion of the patriarchs was appropriated by the warlords. They then took over the priesthood in order to enslave the minds of the Jews. Ten of the tribes were lost. Did they disperse into the rest of the world to get away from the domineering warlords? Maybe they refused to be bullied by the priests. They were the innocents who were sacrificed in battle. Maybe they just wised up to the ways of the bully who used their own religion against them.

I also believe in a God of creativity. A God who creates something out of nothing. Or better said, out of what appears to us to be nothing. We follow in his image. Let me give you an example. Our thoughts are unseen, yet they have power. The Way creates a "spirit" of community amongst its members. As our bodies have separate parts that work together for the whole, so does the Way. We respect the rights and the functions of all of our brothers and sisters in the world. It is unwritten and does not make everyone the same. We revel in our dif-

The Teachings of the Way

ferences. We enjoy our differences. Trade between us reflects one part's ability to supply another with things we could not get otherwise. The contract between us should be the unwritten contract of love. We are not naturally this way. We naturally are creatures of fear and war. All you have to do is look at history. The Way believes in the hope of mankind being able to create a spirit that binds us together, for we all came from one source. We do not preach unity. We preach community.

A voice: Jesus, what is Faith?

Jesus: Faith is bringing into reality things hoped and prayed for. Prayer is answered when we get up off our hands and knees and do something about our problems. Noah built a boat. The Savior Melchizedek performed operations on people to save them from maladies of the body. He experimented with herbs and plants to, perhaps, cure people of disease. Faith is heading out into the uncertain in the service of mankind. If we merely lead passive lives and succumb to the rule of the Romans and brainwashing religion, we never live our own lives. Faith is casting away fear and experimenting for the betterment of human lives.

A voice: How can we separate ourselves from the Roman and religious dominators?

Jesus: We have the vehicle. It is our common spirit of the Way. We outnumber the dominators by a wide margin. The Way does not believe in war. The teachers of war treat it as inevitable and we, the meek and innocent, bear the brunt of its cruelty. If we, the meek and the innocent, stick together all over the world, we shall inherit the earth. It is just as much ours as it is theirs. We must never resort to violence, as it is self-fulfilling. That does not mean that we cannot defend ourselves

The Story of the Savior, Jesus of Nazareth

as Abram did when he went to recover Lot. Violence begets violence.

Another voice: Jesus, did I hear you say that you were a "Son of God?"

Jesus: Absolutely! Furthermore all Peacemakers are Sons of God, because we carry out through our own free will the Way he wants the Universe to be.

The same voice: The Jews say that making yourself like God is a sin.

Jesus: Please remember that the Levites became the priests. The Levites were men of war and were more interested in blind obedience. They promulgated the Rules of War. They were more interested in a population that did as they said. I come to tell you that is not the Way, to blindly follow the whims of the so-called leaders. We must repulse them, but non-violently. Today, all that's left of the twelve tribes are the Sons of the Levites and the Sons of Judah. The other ten tribes are lost.

The spies had heard enough and slipped quietly away from the crowd.

Chapter Twenty-Two
Out of Bondage

The same day at the High Priest's chambers.

High Priest: Well, Judas, what have you learned?

Judas: I and my cohorts here, who can back me up, have been to many meetings of the Way. They plan a conspiracy, a revolution of sorts, against not only our Jewish religion, but the Romans.

High Priest: Well done. We must take action quickly. We must nip this in the bud before the Romans destroy Jerusalem. Pilate will take over if we can find a way to arrest this Jesus of Nazareth. We must keep the crowds out of this, lest we have an insurrection. I would lose my job and maybe worse. What specific charges can I level at him?

Judas: Here's one to think about. Jesus talks as if he were the Son of God. He talks against the High Priest, and the Mosaic Law. What to you think men?

Judas looks to three other spies.

Spy #1: Yes, of course, he has no right to do this by our Laws. What is the penalty?

Spy #2: If I'm not mistaken the penalty is death.

Spy #3: Yes, he should be stoned to death.

The Story of the Savior, Jesus of Nazareth

High Priest: Now, now - all we want to do is turn him over to Pilate for him to do the dirty work. We must wash our hands of this. I will send a letter, marked urgent, to Pilate today. He has the soldiers to implement the plan.

The High Priest wrote a scathing letter and Pilate returned a letter that said he needed to know the whereabouts of this Jesus, so that he might send a detachment of soldiers to arrest him.

High Priest (in his chambers talking to his right hand man): Go fetch Judas. Tell him that Pilate needs to know the whereabouts of Jesus and he will send soldiers to arrest him.

The slithering Judas had spies all over the city. It wasn't long before one had located Jesus and a message was sent to Pilate. To be precise, the soldiers must deliver Jesus to the High Priest for questioning first. Then the High Priest would hand over Jesus to Pilate, with instructions as to what crimes had been committed and the penalty in Jewish Law. Pilate would then carry out the sentence. Since Jesus' rebellion was against the Romans, not his fellow Jews, the High Priest felt that any backlash would go against the Romans.

James, Anne, Mary, Levi, Aaron, Isaac, Thomas, and Jesus were having dinner at a friend's home in Jerusalem. They were talking and laughing and enjoying the meal when there came a rap on the front door. The friend, a high-ranking Pharisee yet sympathetic to new thought, Nicodemus, rose from the table and went to the door.

Nicodemus (after opening the door): What would you like with me? I have done no wrong.

Out of Bondage

Roman soldier: We are here to see one Jesus of Nazareth, upon orders from the Roman Prefect. We have a signed warrant here. (He unrolls a scrolled document).

The diners overhear the conversation. James rushes to the back door and opens it. Two Roman soldiers with drawn swords stare him in the eye; he closes the door.

Nicodemus: I am a high-ranking member of the Temple; surely you have made a mistake.

The Roman soldier: I bring with me a Jewish citizen to identify one Jesus of Nazareth. We have a warrant for his arrest. Let me come in, or we will enter with force.

Nicodemus: We have nothing to hide. We were merely enjoying dinner with friends.

The Roman soldier: Enough!

He brushes by Nicodemus, with part of his entourage - two soldiers and the spy Judas. The soldier approaches the diners - still seated, but all with worried looks.

The Roman soldier (to Judas): Which one is he?

Judas: That one there next to the young woman. (Judas points to Jesus sitting next to Mary, who clutches his hand in hers.)

The Roman soldier: I have here (he unrolls the document) an order for your arrest. You can come with me peacefully. Or we will take you by force. I have several more soldiers outside who spoil for a fight.

The Story of the Savior, Jesus of Nazareth

Jesus rises from his chair. Mary is now sobbing. Jesus does not want to endanger anyone.

James: May I look at the document? (Speaking to the soldier holding it and doing all the talking.)

The Roman soldier: Certainly, but be hasty.

James walks over and peers at the grisly document. His heart is pounding. He feels clammy.

James, after reading, nods to the group an affirmative signal. It's true, as if they didn't already know.

Jesus: I go peacefully.

Out the door they go. Roman authority, talked about for all these years, is materializing in a way unforeseen. The Way was just rolling up a head of steam. James knows they are a resilient bunch. They will get out of this somehow.

The Roman soldiers bring Jesus to the High Priest's meeting room at the Temple. Several of the High Priest's yes men were there.

The High Priest: So you are the one who gives us all this trouble. You look harmless, here all alone. You will need your God to save you now. The Romans are furious. Don't you understand their power? Don't you understand that we are trying to save the Jewish people and Arabs who live here from a violent end? You bit off too big a morsel young man. You shall now choke on it.

Jesus was silent, but looked right at the High Priest.

Out of Bondage

The High Priest (again): You have nothing to say for yourself?

All the High Priest's henchmen stared at Jesus. The Roman soldiers stood at attention and looked straight ahead. Maybe they were listening. Maybe they were thinking about getting drunk later, or chasing some beautiful young Jewish or Arab woman in Jerusalem on off-hours.

The High Priest: Guards! Take this man to the animal pens and scourge him. He will pass out and sleep with the animals for the night. Put him in chains lest he escape. I will deal with him in the morning.

Jesus thought that perhaps if he could withstand the scourging, they would then release him the next morning, thinking they had scared him enough to shut him up. He would have to be much more careful in the future. These men were serious about their power.
The short whips the Roman Guards used on Jesus contained tiny bits of sharp rock imbedded in the leather. They tied him to the front door of a pen full of old mules that were going to be used for animal sacrifice. His head was draped over the top of the pen door so that he could look at the animals as he was lashed. He knew they were sending him a message. He asked the young men, "Who are you? How can you do this to me?" One wouldn't talk. The other merely said, "orders."
The pain was severe and unrelenting. Jesus passed out after perhaps twenty lashes from each soldier. How many they delivered he will never know. He woke up the next morning with ankle chains, tied to the pen. He was lying in straw amongst the animal dung. A soldier approached.

Soldier: Get up! We take you to your appointment now.

The Story of the Savior, Jesus of Nazareth

Jesus (thinks "what appointment?"): Where are you taking me?

The guard swiped Jesus in the mouth with his sword blocker on his left forearm. The swipe knocked two of his teeth out, and blood was now coming from his mouth. As he moved, his back burned intensely and it hurt to move at all. He thought of Mary cleansing his back with pure water and then applying some sort of soothing oil. She would stroke his head and tell him things would be all right.

The Roman soldiers tied a rope around his neck and pulled him forward; otherwise Jesus might dally because of the acute pain. He scuffled along, the chains around his ankles made walking all the more difficult. Fortunately, they put him in a donkey-drawn cart and brought him to Pilate's Jerusalem chambers - amidst gawking spectators. "Who is that poor fool?" they thought. "Pilate is providing another example to discourage dissent." They knew full well what was coming, and soon. Pilate's judgment was swift.

Jesus stood before Pilate. He was a sorry sight. Pilate, on the other hand, smelled like flowers. He had just bathed. His hair, short-cropped and combed forward on the sides, still looked wet. He had several gold rings and bracelets. His tunic was to mid-thigh. His clothing was fresh and clean. His slaves made sure he had fresh clothing at least twice per day. He detested smelling like the common people of Jerusalem. He was their local ruler. He had gotten rid of his wife on one of her frequent trips to Rome. She hated Jerusalem. It was smelly and not as clean as Rome. The people were not of her caliber. Pilate hoped his tenure in Jerusalem would be a stepping-stone to a high-ranking job in the government hierarchy. He had rival Prefects in other provinces that were Roman protectorates. He was well aware that he needed to do things to be noticed by the higher-ups. Stamping out uprisings in the provinces got favorable publicity with the higher-ups in Rome. Collecting more

Out of Bondage

taxes and spending less of Rome's money was crucial. Finding ways to have the locals fund their own improvements would get you ahead. Since his wife was in Rome, he had enjoyed a lovely young Jewish lady the night before. He had a gorgeous Arab woman lined up for tonight's festivities. His work now with this revolutionary had all been pre-planned. All Pilate had to do now was execute his plan. Then most of his afternoon would be free.

Pilate: So you are the one who gathers the throngs! Your work over the past three years has infuriated your religious leaders. They are losing followers left and right. They lose money and cannot help me fund projects to maintain and enhance Jerusalem. What have you got to say for yourself?

Jesus remained silent; not thinking this sordid mess would go this far.

Pilate: Come now, young man, surely you want to get out of here and back to your friends. I have no desire to have your blood on my hands, but I must honor the contract I have with the Jewish leaders.

Jesus thought, what leaders? His liaison was with the Levites, the priestly leaders of the Pharisees and Sadducees. They are not leaders. They are weaklings who will not stand up to the Roman bullies.

Pilate (again): I have a little idea to get you out of this mess. A large group of your followers has gathered in the street below my balcony. The guards shall wash you up and put fresh clothes on you. Then you can address the crowd. I have written down a few words for you to say. They appear angry with me.

The Story of the Savior, Jesus of Nazareth

With that the guards took Jesus into another room and bathed him and wiped the dried blood from his now swollen mouth. They put a fresh robe on him and removed the chains. When he went on the balcony, his legs would still be tied with a cord short enough so that he could not jump off the balcony. They brought him back in front of Pilate, who now sat at a table writing in Hebrew. He stood up with his document.

Pilate: Jesus, this shall be easy and simple. Hear is what I want you to say for saving your life. (He held the document up.) "Ladies and Men of Jerusalem here to support me, I have had a change of mind after serious review with the Prefect's office. He and I think we can work closely together to further the Roman efforts to help the people of Jerusalem. I encourage you to render unto God what is God's and unto Caesar what is Caesar's."

Jesus read it and almost vomited. This sly fox will not interfere with my destiny. He cannot have my mind, too. Perhaps if I incite my followers Pilate will fear for his safety and I can bargain with him.

Pilate: Time is wasting Jesus; your moment of truth arrives. Guards, usher him out to the balcony now.

The soldiers did so. They nudged Jesus out, so that he looked right into the blinding sun. He squinted and could see below a throng of hundreds. "Jesus, Jesus!" they chanted.

Pilate walked out on the balcony and held up his hands. He, too, squinted. He held up both hands.

Pilate: Please, please! Quiet down! I have here Jesus of Nazareth, who is ready to work for the local Roman Prefect and

Out of Bondage

the Roman Empire to help you people of Jerusalem. He has something to say. Say it now or its over, Jesus.

Jesus (haltingly, at first, shouted out with all his might): You must not be intimidated by this bully. (Jesus felt good at his decision to not cave in.) The Way will lead us out of their bondage; we will be free of the war-maker forever. Liberty for the people! Liberty!

Pilate (his eyes meet those of the Savior): You have chosen unwisely, Jesus.

Voices from the crowd: Who is this troublemaker? We don't want trouble. Get rid of him.

Jesus' head is spinning, how could my friends say this?

The soldiers went out to the balcony, ready to push Jesus back in.

Pilate (shouting): He has committed offenses against The Jewish leaders that are punishable by death. What shall I do with him? I have washed my hands of his fate.

The crowd's voices: Execute him! Kill him!

The soldiers pulled Jesus back in. He is confused and shaken.

Pilate: Those people were on my payroll, Jesus. You lost; I won. Perhaps others will think twice before disrupting the order of society that we try so hard to maintain.

Pilate (to the guards): Scourge him once more. Make him carry his own cross to the top of Golgotha. He will roast in the mid-day sun. If his followers dare resurface, we will deal with them at that time. Meanwhile, I will not miss my mid-afternoon swim.

The guards, always acting under orders, carried out without remorse Pilate's nefarious plan. He would take credit for the execution with his Roman bosses and be praised. The locals would blame it on the Jews. Very few knew the reality of the situation.

Nicodemus felt terrible about the crucifixion. Afterwards, he removed Jesus' body from the cave in which it had been placed. He brought it to Qumran, where they buried Jesus properly next to his library.

James, Anne, Mary, and the others of the family of the Way mourned for many days. When the dust settled, they would visit Jesus' mother in Nazareth. They would continue the mission of the Way - to wrest control of the world from the Sons of Darkness.

THE END

Look, next, for Book Two in the Trilogy: *The Story of Saul of Tarsus*, who became the Apostle Paul.

To order this book, contact:

Bristlecone Publishing Co.
2560 Brookridge Ave
Golden Valley, Mn. 55422.
E-mail: davej@jblcompanies.com